Hooked
by the Spirit

Hooked
by the Spirit

Journey

of a

peaceful activist

Rita J. Steinhagen, CSJ

Published by the Sisters of St. Joseph of Carondelet
St. Paul Province
St. Paul, Minnesota
csjstpaul.org

Front cover art: The shimmering fish comes from the artistry of Ansgar Holmberg, CSJ, who says, "The fish is Rita who swallowed the Spirit hook, line, and sinker!"

Dedicated to
The Sisters of St. Joseph of Carondelet, St. Paul Province,
with love and gratitude.

Hooked By The Spirit

You hear the sound it makes
But you do not know where it comes from,
    Or where it goes.
So it is with everyone begotten of the Spirit.

John 3:8

I believe that everyone is "begotten of the Spirit," but we are blown in many different directions. In trying to capture the reason for my many wanderings, I can only surmise that the Spirit assigned to me had an extra wandering gene, which at times caused Her to push, lead, or entice me to places I never dreamed of going. She has been a faithful traveling companion, and I am so grateful She was assigned to me.

Please don't try to figure this out theologically.

Relax. Go with it. Enjoy.

Rita J. Steinhagen, CSJ

Contents

Preface

Who are the people who can spur on a reluctant writer? Or, more to the point, who are the people who can get a non-writer to write? The first suggestion that I should write a book came many years ago from Sister Antonine O'Brien, CSJ, who was retired and living at the retirement home of the Sisters of St. Joseph. She stopped me in a hallway and asked me if I was writing. She might as well have asked me if I had visited Mars lately.

Years later I was asked that same question by my friend, Emmanuel Renner, OSB, at the Monastery of St. Benedict. "Are you writing?" she asked. "You are at Timberlee now (our sisters' vacation spot), so you have time. Write!" So I did. I wrote one or two whole pages—and that was that.

The third time I was told to write came after I was released from prison in September 1998. My CSJ friends Catherine Litecky and Eleanor Lincoln told me to write and offered to be my editors and strongly urged me to write.

Our timetables often did not match but my editors hung with me. With much pushing and prodding, for over five years, the results are now in your hands. I owe both of them incalculable gratitude, for without them I doubt I ever would have written this book. Thank you, Catherine and Eleanor, for your persistence—and for your belief that my story was worth telling.

There are many other people who gave of their time and talents to make this book possible. I thank them all with a big, big thank you.

Ansgar Holmberg, CSJ, the artist who created the book's magnificent cover. I am amazed that Ansgar is still well and happy. I nearly drove her crazy by changing the title of the book every week.

Ann Thompson, the communications director for our community, gave me extremely valuable assistance. She gave the titles to the chapters of the book and often provided insightful comments and suggestions. With her associate Jan Zitnick, they produced the layout, including pictures and fishing hooks. Ann and Jan also helped coordinate the printing of the book.

Mary Jo Richardson, Deb Chernick, Joan Mitchell, CSJ, and Helen Coughlan, CSJ, were encouraging and had questioning comments about my writing that were very helpful. My neighbor, Carolyn Wavrin, also gave me invaluable feedback.

Many people allowed me to use their photos: Tom Bottolene, Chris Spotted Eagle, Marlys Weber, and CSJs Sylvia Krawfcyk, Dolore Rochon, Baya Clare, and Mary Kay Kottenstette.

Sister Emmanuel, who at long last, has read the fruit of her early promptings has given me a "thumbs up," and Sister Colman O'Connell, OSB, made an insightful suggestion—that I emphasize that my wanderings have been a "spiritual journey of God leading a listening heart" and not because I was "unstable." I hope that that possibility has been settled favorably.

With the expertise of Carol Masters the book had its final "going over."

Finally, thanks to the numerous people who kept asking, "How is your book coming? When will it be done?" Perhaps it was these questions—in addition to my tenacious editors—that kept me going.

It is a very good feeling to say IT IS DONE!

Rita J. Steinhagen, CSJ

Foreword

Henry David Thoreau had it that many people "go fishing all their lives without knowing that it is not fish they are after!" Not so our Rita. Thoreau would like her. As the chapters of her life say so clearly, down the years she's been catching more than her "limit" of wisdom and mercy and then "multiplying" the catch a hundredfold with us all.

Take her prison chapter. If Henry could have seen her in prison, he would probably recall to her a conversation from jail that he had with his pal, Ralph Emerson, who quipped: "What are you doing in there?" To which Henry replied, "What are you doing out there?"

Rita was in good company. Jesus crossed the line, too, and landed in jail for confronting a system of domination and exploitation (John 18:10). She's been imitating Jesus as long as I've known her. In that chapter, like Jesus, she didn't want any Peters among us cutting off ears to keep her out of prison. She did want people to "see" and "hear" an evil the courts and the military were covering up.

When I visited her in prison, she was herself, beautiful as ever, funny, focused, furious, and simultaneously as deep as the sea. All of her chapters mix the everyday stuff like bugs and ashtrays with the empathy she feels because she hears the depth of human pain and suffering. She lowers her "line" into people's hearts—from her depths to their depths. Compassion invariably follows. What also follows is her prophetic and impassioned crying out: Change the unjust systems.

Reading her story sends us into our depths pondering the growing violence in our homes and streets and sports and foreign policy. We hear her Jesus crying out, "The measure with which you measure will be measured back to you."

We thank God for Rita. We thank Rita. Her measure is mercy. She keeps "catching up" our hearts in her net. We learn from her how to cry out, too.

Moreover, we learn from her word and her deeds the peace and the wisdom that come from quiet fishing, even in the midst of stormy seas or streets or prisons. Haunted both by God and by injustice, she lives her CSJ promise to love God and neighbor without distinction. Somehow her soul stays aware not only of deep pain but also of deep beauty and deep connection. Somehow, at the heart of the matter is her faith that at the heart of all matters is God breathing love.

We stay tuned to see where that quiet passion will take her next.

Char Madigan, CSJ

Introduction

Sister Rita Steinhagen, CSJ, has quite a story to tell.

Unassuming and introspective, she has reached out to segments of society many people ignore. And, as one friend said about her resilient life, "One thing has led to another."

Rita, like all visionaries, has continually heard "the cry of the poor." From a totally unexpected call to religious life as a Sisters of St. Joseph of Carondelet when she was 23 years old to being sentenced to prison on her 70th birthday, Rita has reached beyond herself in compassionate action.

She was welcomed by the hippies on the West Bank of Minneapolis in the early 1970s. At the Free Store that she operated on the West Bank, she encountered not only the physical but also the spiritual needs of many who were poor, lonely, disturbed. At the request of a runaway who spent her days and nights on the street, she established The Bridge, a shelter for runaway youth. The Bridge is still functioning in Minneapolis more than 35 years later.

To renew her contemplative spirit, Rita spent the next two years as a core member of a newly established house of prayer in Stillwater, Minnesota, sponsored by her religious community. In Rita the characteristics of both Martha and Mary of the gospel story find balance.

In the spirit of Dorothy Day, her inspiration, Rita, with Char Madigan, CSJ, turned her efforts to begin a house of hospitality for women and children. They opened the doors of St. Joseph House, which today continues to flourish and expand as Hope Community, a model development of inner city renewal on Portland Avenue in Minneapolis.

Because many of the people she met in her ministries spoke Spanish, Rita, who had decided it was time to learn the language, went to Spanish language school in El Paso, Texas. After completing her studies, she remained in El Paso to work with refugees. Hearing the stories of those fleeing the war in

Central America, Rita became a long-term volunteer with Witness for Peace, a group of Americans committed to living in the danger zones in Nicaragua to give support and protection to the people suffering from the effect of the Contra war. This profound experience led her, when she returned to Minneapolis, to serve for seven years as a volunteer at the Center for Victims of Torture.

She became increasingly involved in peace and justice causes. Haunted by her experiences of learning about the results of torture throughout the world and knowing about the U.S. complicity in training Central American soldiers in methods of torture, she participated in peaceful demonstrations against the School of the Americas at Fort Benning, Georgia.

Her protests there eventually led to a six-month sentence in a Federal Prison and a $3,000 fine for the misdemeanor of crossing a line into Fort Benning. Her time in prison called her to an expanded view of peace and justice in a troubled world, especially the need for prison reform.

Many women in the Federal Prison in Pekin, Illinois, believed that she was sent there for their benefit. One of the women, sent to prison for the same reason as Rita, said of her, "Sister Rita has a presence which is built on her long life of faith, and the inmates of all ages trusted her."

While in prison, Rita, the contemplative, kept a journal and wrote poetry. In one of her haikus, she seems to be describing her own indomitable but gentle spirit:

> Fluffs of cottonwood
> Sailing upward in blue sky
> In prison but free.

Rita's prison experience opened up a new focus for her life. Her friends predicted that she would aim to reform the system and that, indeed, is her current call.

We and her other friends have persuaded her to write her story as an act of social justice.

Eleanor Lincoln, CSJ and Catherine Litecky, CSJ
Professors Emeritae, The College of St. Catherine and
Co-directors of Women at the Well

1

Beginnings

I've found that events or happenings in life seldom, if ever, occur in isolation. Most often our lives have a common thread running through them. We are changed and formed by the people we meet, the books we read, and the experiences we have. An accident or a major medical diagnosis can be life-changing—and give life greater depth and meaning.

In Walden Pond Henry Thoreau wrote, "I went to the woods because I wished to live deliberately,...and not when I came to die, discover that I had not lived.... I wanted to live deep and suck out all the marrow of life." I can't say that I made such a conscious decision, as Thoreau did, "to live deliberately." For me, things just happened.

I came into the world at midnight on a Saturday in the middle of a January blizzard. I was born at home in Waconia, Minnesota, a small German town about 35 miles west of the Twin Cities. On Sunday morning I was bundled up and taken to the church of St. Joseph to be baptized after Mass. (To this day I can't imagine doing such a thing.) My godparents, Helen and Rufinus, an aunt and uncle from the farm, thought the roads would soon be blocked, so I was baptized while they were in town for Mass.

My father's side of the family. In front, from left, are my great-grandmother Anna Henke and my grandmother, Mary Jane Steinhagen. Behind them, from left, are me, my father Joseph, my brother David, and my sister Lois. This photo was taken in 1940 or 1941.

My Dad and Mom, Joseph and Ruth, share a good story. I wish I knew what it was.

I was the second child and second girl born to my parents, Ruth and Joseph Steinhagen. My older sister, Lois, had been born three and a half years earlier in Hallock, Minnesota, where my father was a banker and my mother taught grade school. It was the time of the Great Depression, and my father had the job of closing banks. My parents then moved to Waconia, my father's hometown, where I was born and where my father got into the telephone business. Now an independent telephone exchange owner, my father kept his family and business moving to keep ahead of the Bell Telephone Company, which was buying up small telephone exchanges. From Waconia he moved our family to Bertha, Minnesota, where my brother, David, was born when I was four years old.

We didn't live in Bertha very long. By the time I started grade school, we had moved to Deer Creek. I have happy and vivid memories of that small town of 200 people.

Our home on Main Street had a large fenced-in yard where the Methodist women held their ice cream socials. The town pump across the street had a large wooden tub under its spout filled with water. There in the evenings we kids would have water fights.

In Waconia with my dad Joseph and my older sister Lois. I am about age two.

My second-grade class. I am sitting—quite unlady-like—in the front row second from the right.

The blacksmith shop, not far from the pump, had a wide, open door where kids gathered to watch Mr. Moody pound red-hot horseshoes as sparks flew. (That scene comes back to me whenever I read the poem The Village Blacksmith.)

Behind our house and across the alley was the skating rink/ball park. When my mother wanted us kids home, she stood on the back porch and rang a cowbell. Other kids would holler, "It's time for the cows to go home." Soon, however, their mothers told them, "When Mrs. Steinhagen rings the cowbell, you come home too."

My mother sewed most of our clothes. When I brought home a friend whose coat was fastened with a safety pin, it was off with the coat and on with a button.

We were the only Catholic family in town, but the Mose family, who farmed, were also Catholic. Sunday Mass and Saturday catechism were held in Bluffton, Minnesota, 11 miles to the north. Every other Saturday my dad or Mr. Mose drove a car packed with kids to catechism class in Bluffton.

I hated the days that Mr. Mose drove. His old Chevy reeked of gasoline, his boots smelled of manure, and he smoked a cigar. I was so sick by the time the car door opened in Bluffton that I was in no shape to learn anything. Then we piled back in the car again for another 11 miles of terrible smells.

I finished fifth grade in Deer Creek, Minnesota, but hadn't made my first communion yet, so we moved to Walker, Minnesota, in time for me to enroll in the summer catechism class. Walker is where I put down roots, and where Lois, our

Me, Lois, and David in Deer Creek. The next year we moved to Walker.

cousin Colleen, and I finished high school. Colleen had come to live with us during her high school years.

Walker was a good town in which to grow up. There were no cliques or "in" or "out" circles. We were all good friends who enjoyed ice skating, biking, fishing, dancing, swimming, high school sports, and cherry Cokes. My high school class-mates became lifelong friends. It was in Walker that I learned to fish.

After her graduation, Lois entered nurses training at St. Mary's Hospital in Rochester, Minnesota. Colleen got mar-ried, and David finished high school in Morgan because my folks continued to move to keep ahead of Ma Bell. When my family moved to Morgan in 1945, I stayed behind because I was a patient at the Minnesota State Sanatorium for Tuberculosis, located three miles from

After fishing off the city dock in Walker, my broth-er David helps me dis-play the catch of the day: two nice walleyes from Leech Lake!

Walker at Ah-Gwah-Ching. In my junior year of high school I was one of three stu-dents diagnosed with tuberculosis. I spent 11 months at the sana-torium, from February of my junior year to January of my senior year—a gap that really messed up my high school years. After I was discharged from the sanatorium, I lived in Walker with my good friend and class-mate, Loie, and graduated with my class.

In high school, I looked a bit more serious.

From Morgan my parents moved to Dodge Center, Minnesota, and then Brooten, Minnesota, before returning to Dodge Center when they retired. In their retirement years, my parents continued their interest in antiques, mom with her trivets, butterpats, and antique furniture, and dad with his collection of old powder flasks and a few muskets. He also made small steam engines that he drove around town with a stream of kids following him.

After I finished high school, while I was visiting my parents in Dodge Center, a fellow came to the door recruiting students for a small school in Minneapolis that offered medical courses. I had never thought of entering such a field, but it sounded interesting, so I took the course in medical technology and later worked in the laboratory at the sanatorium where I had been a patient. There I met students from the College of St. Catherine in St. Paul, Minnesota, who were doing internship work at the sanatorium.

When one of these students joined the Sisters of St. Joseph of Carondelet (CSJ) in St. Paul, I went to visit her. While I was waiting for her in the convent parlor, the director of novices chatted with me. How the course of our conversation progressed the way it did still remains a mystery to me. Even more of a mystery is the question I asked her: "Do you think I belong here?"

"I certainly do," she said.

Three months later, at age 23, I amazed myself and everybody who knew me by joining a new group of postulants at the Sisters

In 1951, I was a postulant. My mother wrote on the back of this photo, "Slacks spoiled her poise. She's learning how to sit." I'm still learning!

of St. Joseph convent. Never having attended a Catholic school and having had no contact with sisters except for a two-week summer catechism class, I knew next to nothing about who sisters were or what they did.

My first night at the convent—February 2, 1951—was the Feast of Candlemas (the feast of lights). Everyone carried a lighted candle as we walked through the halls. I remember thinking, "So this is what sisters do, parade around the halls at night with candles." I soon realized that this was a once-a-year celebration.

Before long, life settled into a daily routine of prayer, work, study, and recreation. My call to religious life had been a bit unusual, but religious life for me has been a lasting, challenging, and happy one.

Later I learned that some in the convent had had doubts about my future as a religious sister. When I entered as a postulant, a novice was assigned as my "big sister" to help me adjust to convent living. We were supposed to sew numbers on our clothes for identification at the laundry. Mother Bertha, mistress of postulants, told the novice, "Don't have Rita sew on all of her numbers—she won't be staying anyway."

From my point of view, I felt like a fish that had finally found water. A whole new world opened up for me that I hadn't known existed—the spiritual world. I eagerly read not only the Bible but spiritual writers such as Dom Columba Marmion, Thomas Merton, Gerald Vann, Leon Bloy, St. Teresa of Avila, Caryll

I found a lake somewhere that produced a northern and a small bass.

Houselander, Hubert Van Zeller, Jessica Powers, and a host of others.

I completed my novitiate training and took my vows in 1953. After completing my college degree and state exams in medical technology, I was assigned to the laboratory at St. Michael's Hospital in Grand Forks, North Dakota.

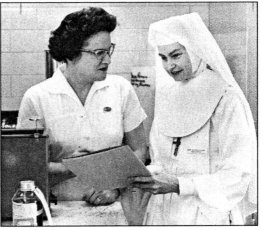

In 1956, I was assigned to St. Michael's Hospital in Grand Forks. For 10 years I ran the lab and loved every minute of it. Instructor Jean Saumner visited occasionally.

Occasionally I went to the Newman Center, which was located a short distance from the hospital. One day while I was there, I picked up a copy of The Catholic Worker newspaper. For the first time I became acquainted with Dorothy Day, editor of this paper and co-founder of the Catholic Worker movement. Learning about Dorothy Day was the spark that lit my social consciousness.

In the newspaper I saw a request for old clothing. I don't think that I had ever really thought about poor people before, having come from a small town where there was little real poverty. The Catholic Worker showed me a different side of life.

I tacked up a note in the hospital asking doctors and nurses to contribute to the cause and soon sent off a huge box of clothing to New York. I laugh when I remember that now. The Catholic Worker house would have been further ahead if I had sent them the postage money.

Yet, sending boxes of old clothes to Dorothy Day at the Catholic Worker house was probably as far as my small flame of social consciousness would have gone had it not been for a medical diagnosis that changed my life drastically.

After running the laboratory at St. Michael's Hospital for ten years and training students from the University of North Dakota in their internship year, I was transferred to Trinity Hospital in Jamestown, North Dakota.

It was there, in 1966, at age 37, I was diagnosed with multiple sclerosis. The doctor told me I would probably be in a wheelchair in ten years. I knew that as the disease progressed, I couldn't remain in the lab work that I loved, so I sought retraining in another field.

At that time my community was seeking teachers for the instructional program for young sisters. Knowing that I could teach from a wheelchair if that day came, I went back to the College of St. Catherine to take theology and scripture courses. I soon realized that I couldn't keep up physically, having to walk the distances between the buildings on campus, so I dropped out of college.

One of my sister friends, a medical technologist, invited me to live with her and three other sisters of my community living in the Cedar-Riverside area of Minneapolis. One day I mentioned to one of my new housemates that I wanted to work with the poor but didn't know how to get started. She told me that Father Harry Bury of the University of Minnesota's Newman Center often put notices in the St. Francis Cabrini church bulletin asking for clothing and small household articles for the Free Store, a store where donated articles were given without charge to those in need.

When I called Father Bury, he invited me to a meeting with him and other University campus ministers. This group of ministers, the sponsors of the Free Store, was delighted to have me help out. I was soon introduced to the Cedar-Riverside area of Minneapolis by Bill Teska, an Episcopalian deacon.

Little did I realize then how the small flame lit by Dorothy Day would simmer into a gradual, accumulated awareness that would burn throughout my life—a life that has been much longer and richer than the doctors or I could have imagined.

2

The Free Store
The Hippie Nun

The hippie movement was in full swing when I arrived on Cedar Avenue in December 1968. A whole new world opened up to me. I was a woman religious, dressed in a "modified habit" consisting of a dark skirt, white blouse, and short veil. I don't know who got the bigger jolt, the hippies or me, but we not only accepted one another, we also enjoyed each other.

Because of my multiple sclerosis, at times I had difficulty walking. But I was lucky that the location of the Free Store was in the busy part of Cedar Avenue. I parked my old car in the store parking lot and slowly walked the street and introduced myself to the hippies. "Cool," said a young woman called Furry Foot. "It will be good to have you in the area."

The area was called Cedar-Riverside or the West Bank because the University of Minnesota expanded to the west side of the Mississippi River close to the intersection of Cedar Avenue and Riverside Avenue. This older part of the city had a good mix of businesses: a drug store, an art supply store, a meat market, a bank, two or three small cafes, a bakery, a dance and performing arts center, a metal and leather art shop, a liquor store, and a few bars. Dulcimers were made on the second floor of one of the shops.

Among these buildings was the storefront rented by the campus ministry group, made up of several denominations. The store accepted donated articles such as clothing and small household articles given without charge to those in need. When I first saw it, the store was dark, dirty, and empty except for a few empty clothes racks and a big cardboard box filled with dirty old clothes sitting in the middle of the room. The campus ministry group hoped to open the store at a new location, a couple of blocks south on the corner of Sixth Street and Cedar Avenue.

Subsequently I learned that the health officials and police had closed the store because it had not been consistently staffed and had turned into a warming house for winos, drug addicts, and runaways. The landlords, owners of both buildings, were not eager to rent to campus ministry again because of the problems at the store. My job would be to convince the landlords that I could run the new place efficiently. I would open and close the store each day, and I would be there during the hours it was open.

For three months I continued to try to convince the landlords that I would be responsible for the building, but they were reluctant to give me a key; however, the months of waiting until I got the key in March gave another boost to my education. The landlords, Keith Heller and Gloria Siegal, owned many rental units in the Cedar-Riverside area and employed social workers to check on renters who were sick or elderly. Many of the buildings would eventually be razed by Heller and Siegal to construct new housing. It was good public relations to make sure that the people living in those units were taken care of. I made rounds with Sue, one of the social workers, and soon became acquainted with several of the residents.

Mike Downy became my favorite. He lived in a small room on the second floor of an old house that was soon to be demolished. The first time I met him he was sitting on the side of his rumpled bed. On the floor stood several tin cans filled with urine. His cane leaned against the wall. He had a beard and sparkling, piercing eyes, and although he was ill he did not want to go to the hospital.

He finally agreed that he would go with Sue and me to Hennepin General Hospital on the following Monday. When we came to his room on Monday, he was sitting on the edge of his bed with his hat and cane next to him ready to go. A month later when he was discharged from the hospital, we got him an apartment above the Brite Spot bar. This was a bad choice—too many stairs—so we moved him to the Cedar Pines Nursing Home.

His needs were few: a calendar in January and a fly swatter in June. But Mike did miss his friends on Cedar Avenue, so periodically I drove him to the Pilots Club on Seventh and Cedar so he could have a beer or two with his old buddies.

Mike had wit and humor. From him I learned much about the inner workings of a nursing home as well as the detailed activities of all neighbors within view of his window.

After further bouts of illness and hospitalization, Mike died. I arranged with a local priest to have a service for him at the mortuary. Two sister friends went with me. I prayed beside Mike's coffin words from Psalm 103:15-16:

Man's days are like grass:
like a flower in the field he blooms:
The wind sweeps over him and he is gone
and his place knows him no more.

Of the four people gathered around his coffin, I was the only one who had known him—and that was only for a short time. Mike was buried in a pauper's grave. I knew nothing of his family. He had spent 70 or 80 years on earth, and no one noted his passing except a few strangers. His life most likely was one of isolation, separation, non-communication, and loneliness. These same realities brought runaway kids to the West Bank by the hundreds.

During this time I continued to negotiate with the landlords about the store. When I had first looked through its dirty windows, I saw the long dusty meat counters and other equipment that were there when it was a grocery store. The landlady said that she would have them removed. I continued to meet with ministers, social workers, landlords, and other community leaders who were concerned about the number of minors on the streets.

Finally, on March 17, 1969, I got the key to the new store. The place was a mess. The floor was filthy, walls needed painting, windows needed washing, and the ceiling hung at odd angles. The dirty meat counters were still there. I rounded up a motley assortment of people—hippies, runaways, women religious, winos, and friends—and we began the cleaning.

In the midst of all of this activity, my ecumenical prayer life began. I attended prayer meetings at a place called Daystar, which welcomed people of all denominations. One morning while there I received a message from a Dr. Judy Bergfalk saying that she would like to meet with me. (Heaven only knows how she tracked me down!)

She had just finished medical school and wanted to work on the West Bank. When we met, I told her that when the place was clean and the partitions were up, I would see to it that she had an office in the back part of the store, and I would make a small area for a laboratory and do the lab work.

A leader in the hippie community invited me to attend one of their monthly meetings. On a cold Sunday afternoon in January, my friend Sister Rose Marie Blazek and I, dressed in our modified habits, went to their meeting. We joined the large circle on the floor in the basement of a former church, now converted to a multipurpose community center. The discussion was about community issues such as what to do with the large number of runaways in the area. After an hour and a half, the meeting ended with a relaxation technique. All of us lay flat on the floor, and the leader in a monotone voice said, "Your toes are relaxing, your feet are relaxing, your ankles are relaxing," and he continued naming body parts that were relaxing all the way up to our heads. And so the meeting ended, everyone flat on the floor— and relaxed!

Periodically the symptoms of my multiple sclerosis showed up as the tingling or numbing of my feet or legs, but my double vision had disappeared. I was functioning very well, and eventually the symptoms disappeared altogether. To this day I have had no recurring problems with the disease.

Sometimes I wonder about that diagnosis and the profound change it made in my life. I know what happened to me happens to other people. A major, unexpected event can forever change a life. And my life certainly was changed.

Progress on the store moved slowly, but eventually there were a new floor and partitions for Dr. Judy's office and a laboratory. By June 1969 the store was in good shape. A jug band played for the open house. It was a grand day for all.

Many people came to volunteer in the store. Two of the first to arrive were Sister Barbara Whitlow and Kathy Niska, a student at the University of Minnesota who had read about the store on a campus bulletin board. Kathy later brought her sister Patty. They staffed the store for the summer months and fit right in with the people on the avenue.

Donations for the store arrived in various ways. One day I found five packages at the back door, each individually wrapped in newspaper and sealed with masking tape. My amazement increased with each unwrapping: a Girl Scout book, a bottle of hand lotion, a dress, hair clippers, and a urinal.

Now that the store was open, it was time to paint the name above the front door. Flip, a very dis turbed young man who was a regular at the store, did have some painting talent. The day he painted our sign he was high on drugs and drunk on wine, but he did a

Flip, although not completely sober, paints the name of the store in nice bold letters.

good job. The name "Free Store" appeared in nice big letters above our front door.

Another regular helper was a conscientious objector from California. The government had assigned him to a clerical job in California, which didn't suit him, so he "disappeared" to Minnesota. One day the FBI came looking for him. I agreed to give the young man the message if I saw him, which I did.

A few days later Willie, who had blown his mind on drugs, was sitting cross-legged on my desk playing a flute. Kelly, another disturbed person who continually wore a construction hard hat, was causing a great commotion. Phillip, who also had his mind permanently altered by drugs, was standing on his head on a couch in the front of the store. In the middle of all this activity in came my conscientious objector friend to call the FBI and turn himself in. North Dakota was never like this.

Meanwhile, the runaways were getting younger, and the other store clientele were getting older. A nine-year-old came in to ask me if he could sleep in the store at night. Sarah and Anna, two elderly women from the high-rise across the street, came in to check me out. They had heard that I was a hippie sister working with the hippies. I told them that I didn't know about being a hippie sister but that everyone was welcome in the store. The high-rise residents became frequent "shoppers."

Besides the local clientele, the store had other interesting visitors—all within one week. Four policewomen who came in together, several women religious, a few bikers (motorcycle gang members), and two health inspectors checking for food (no food was allowed in the store).

What I needed was a van. It could be parked in the lot next to the store and I could distribute bread from the back of it. I also occasionally picked up donations and at times I drove the shoppers home with their full bags and boxes.

To raise money for a van I spoke to the congregation at the Newman Center Masses. I said that I had told God I would drive the van if He would pay for it. I also told the congregation that I thought that God was probably asking a lot of them to help him out. The resulting collection generated enough money for a down payment on a good second-hand van. I borrowed the rest of the money from my community and repaid it bit by bit from the money I received for speaking engagements.

I lived with two other sisters a mile or so from the store, and occasionally a few of the street people arrived at our home, usually at meal time. This made for an interesting extended family and conversation. The conscientious objector from California reminded me that he was coming for supper on Wednesday and that he wanted pork chops. He arrived on Wednesday—with Chris and Dave in tow. Pork chops are a lot harder to multiply than fish and bread.

An amazing variety of people had entered my life since I had come to the West Bank. Some I saw only once or twice, but others who lived in the area became regulars at the store. Elderly people from the high-rise were frequent visitors as were numerous hippies. Some runaways also came in often, particularly those who lived on the roof of a department store on Cedar Avenue.

One of my favorite people on the West Bank, Norman. He was witty, funny, respectful, and addicted to alcohol. I unsuccessfully tried to locate him in 2005.

Of the numerous winos, two of my favorites were Norman and Francis. Norman was a funny, exasperating character who for a time lived with his friend Francis in an abandoned car behind the store—with a mail box perched on top. Norman, at times with a wink, would call Francis "dear" and hastily explain that, although both of them lived in the same old car, one slept in the front seat and the other in the back. Francis would fume. One day when Norman was looking at himself in a mirror in the store, I heard him say, "My golly, you are a good looking guy, but why don't you shape up?" My thoughts exactly.

January 7, 1970, in the cold early morning hours, I got a call that the Sixth Street block of Cedar Avenue was burning. I arrived to find that the Free Store on the corner of that block was safe, but that the bakery/cafe and a former hotel, then serving as a community hangout, were gone. The Free Store, coated with ice, stood glistening like a sad ice sculpture in the morning sun.

The ashes from the buildings that had burned tracked into the Free Store and made a mess. For days Francis scrubbed the floor trying to keep the place clean.

Dr. Judy was now officially seeing patients. Occasionally there was an odd request. One man was bitten by his boa constrictor, which was still loose someplace in his house. A dog hit by a car in front of the Free Store was carried in to Dr. Judy, but the animal was in such bad shape that she could do nothing for it. One of the young men waiting to see the doctor said he would take care of it. He took the dog out behind the store and shot it.

Flip, the man who had painted our Free Store sign and the inside walls of the store (and slopped red paint all over), began shooting up fingernail polish remover and was hospitalized. When I visited him in the hospital mental ward, he told me that he wanted to return to Pennsylvania. After he was released from the hospital, we heard a rumor that he was going to kill Dr. Judy. We quickly rounded up money for a bus ticket to Pennsylvania. I drove him to the bus depot and stayed with him until he boarded the bus.

With all of the problems in the area, including the challenge of running the store, I decided to partition off space in the back of the store for a prayer room. Small as the gatherings usually were, the prayer of those who came was very touching. Some prayed for healing of their addictions. On occasion someone would bring a friend to be prayed for. A fellow who was on crack and had the shakes came to be prayed over. The place was certainly not a Lourdes, but I believe that all prayer brings some type of healing.

Kip, a fellow who came often, asked for prayers that his marriage might work out. He and his wife had separated. His wife came to see me and told me that she was serious about quitting drugs and that she still loved him. One day in July when I went to the Free Store I found a bouquet of roses for me from Kip. He then disappeared from my life until 1998, 28 years later, when I received a letter from him while I was in prison. He and his wife are divorced. He is now living as a recluse in the woods of northern Minnesota, trapping for a living.

John, another hippie who often had 20 to 30 runaways sleeping on mattresses on the floor of his house, came to the store with an unusual request. He wanted a statue of an angel for his house. I would see what I could do.

I called one of our convents (Holy Angels, of course) with his request. Yes, they had an angel stored someplace. Three hippies went with me in the van to get the angel and soon my happy hippie friend had the life-size angel installed on the roof of his front porch. The beauty of it all inspired a local newspaper to publish a picture of the statue and a short article. Inscribed on a wall inside John's house were the opening words of the prayer "Angel of God, my guardian dear." The runaways certainly needed all of the protection they could get.

The sisters I lived with became nervous about some of these activities. The police called at 10 o'clock one night looking for runaways—and me. The sister answering the phone said, "Rita is not home. We don't know where she is or what she does."

The two girls they were looking for had gone home with another woman. I picked them up at her home the next morning and drove them to Legal Aid and the county welfare office.

The social worker there said that the runaways could stay with me during the day, but the police would not agree to the arrangement. That afternoon I drove the girls to the detention center.

People often asked me why I did what I did. Dr. Grace Carlson, a professor at St. Mary's Junior College in Minneapolis, was one who questioned me. As a former member of the Communist Party who had spent time in prison, she had questions on the value, or lack thereof, of what I was doing. We had great discussions.

In essence, her argument was that as long as people handed out food and clothing, the system wouldn't change because "those people" were being taken care of. I responded, "If everyone who was providing these goods stopped tomorrow, there would be a lot of people cold and hungry." I agreed with her that there must be systemic change, but, oh, it comes so slowly. In the meanwhile, I suggested, she should work at one end of the problem and I would work at the other. I used Dr. Carlson's gift of $25 to feed the hungry.

Of course, Dr. Carlson was right, and Dorothy Day would agree with her that something must be done to bring about a better social order based on the teachings of Christ. I agree with Dorothy's statement that "our problems stem from our acceptance of this filthy, rotten system."

Dorothy, herself at one time sympathetic to the Communist Party and no stranger to jails, wrote: "Within the Catholic Worker there has always been such emphasis placed on the works of mercy, feeding the hungry, clothing the naked, sheltering the homeless, that it has seemed to many of our intellectuals a top-heavy performance—it is, in a way, emergency work, the vanguard work that we are doing. Others will come along, and have come along, to go forth from this school of action to work in the adult education movement, the credit union movement, the cooperative movement, to start new schools, to work as teachers, writers, etc., apostles in new fields, wherever God leads them, wherever they find their vocation."

She also believed that the immediate solution of problems will always be the works of mercy, one of which is "sheltering the homeless."

The greatest number of "homeless" I encountered daily were the runaways who came to the Free Store. At one of our community meetings concerning the alarming number of runaways in the area, a hippie named Dave arrived with three runaways in tow. He told us that his place was full. Who would take these kids home for the night? Cindy, a 14-year-old, came home with me. But taking the kids to our homes was not the answer to the enormous problem, and besides it was illegal.

It was one of the runaways who said to me one day, "Why don't you get us a place to stay?" Well, that was a new thought and possibly a good solution.

3

The Bridge
"Get us a place to stay"

At the next meeting of the community leaders, when we were again discussing the runaway problem, I mentioned that if I had a house I would try to get it licensed and take in runaways. Gloria Siegel, Free Store landlord, told me that she and her business partner Keith Heller owned a boarded-up house on 20th Avenue South in Minneapolis. If I thought that the building would work, they would fix it up for me.

In June 1970 I went through the house and found it to be sound and fairly large. It would be fine, and so a house for runaways came to be.

As with all births, the shelter for runaways was not born without pain. In the beginning everything went well. When I told my religious superiors of my plans for a house for the runaways, they were very supportive. They also approved of my asking one of our sisters if she would be interested in working at the house.

I contacted Sister Marlene Barghini, who was just finishing her studies in family counseling at the Menninger Foundation in Topeka, Kansas. She responded to my request to join me with a question. "What's a runaway house?" I told her, "I really don't know, but a large number of runaways in the area need help—professional help—so I'm starting a house for them."

Marlene came, she saw, and she stayed. For 14 years she not only counseled the youth and their parents but arranged a partnership with the University of Minnesota to be a field placement for the University's students in social work.

With the help of Gloria and Keith, the renovation of the house began. Their gift of $7,000 went to fix windows, plumbing, and heating. Their generosity really launched the runaway house.

In June 1970 before our home for runaways opened, the Minneapolis Community Health and Welfare Council formed a committee called the Runaway Assistance Program (RAP). The group reported that more than 5,000 minors had been on the streets in 1969, and RAP was seeking ways to address this problem.

I received a copy of RAP's "confidential report," which said in part, "The current situation regarding the two existing runaway houses, one called Our House and the other Commune, is uncertain, at best. Our House...is not licensed...and cannot be approved or licensed in its present physical condition. The Commune is in equally bad shape if not worse. Its operator is dismissing all runaways while he has gone north to 'find his head.'"

The report went on to say that I was concerned about the runaways and was negotiating with Cedar-Riverside Association about the renovation of a building to make a home and other services available to runaways, especially girls. It stated, "Rita's reputation and credibility on the West Bank is a universally good one with persons of all philosophies and persuasions. We feel she has the charismatic qualities necessary and essential to give credibility and stability to a beginning project of establishing service for runaway youth."

So, with all of that, I had the blessing of the establishment, but I still had to navigate their endless rules and regulations. At one of the many RAP meetings, Father Jerome Boxleitner of Catholic Charities spoke with me about his concern for the funding of the runaway house. He thought it would be easier to get funding if the house was under the umbrella of Catholic Charities, whose name would give the place credibility. I was a bit leery of this arrangement but willing to give it a try.

The house was not yet habitable, so the four of us who would be staffing it (Sisters Mary Joseph "Jo" Wilson, Barbara Jenson, Marlene, and I) moved temporarily into the unoccupied quarters intended for priests at St. Joseph's Home for Children, which was run by Catholic Charities.

My life needed balance, a time for prayer and quiet, so I took a few days off and went to Timberlee, our community's lake place. One evening a sister strummed her guitar and sang, "Like a Bridge Over Troubled Waters." It struck a chord in me. I now had found the name for the runaway house—The Bridge.

Back in Minneapolis I attended meetings, meetings, and more meetings. I met with law enforcement peo-

Repairs are started on The Bridge at 608 - 20th Avenue South in Minneapolis. The generosity of Gloria Siegel and Keith Heller launched The Bridge.

ple, social workers, and fire and building inspectors. I also worked with the Community Health and Welfare committee about funding. The idea for The Bridge was approved, but getting the place functioning was an uphill battle.

The committee and I had a difference of opinion about who the clientele of The Bridge should be. The committee said that funding might not be available if only girls were accepted. I said, "Just girls to start with. Let's live there a few weeks to see where the bedrooms and bathrooms are and if the showers and toilets work."

I thought the hassle of moving into a new place with young girls who had problems would be enough of a challenge without the "boy" factor. Boys could be accepted later when we figured out what we were doing.

Although work on the house had progressed with new windows, plumbing and heating, the fire marshal said that an outside fire exit was needed. Also the three-foot-high wood paneling in the kitchen needed to be replaced by plain sheet rock. A hood was required over the stove.

While the work on The Bridge continued, I worked at the Free Store. I saved the donated pots, pans, and dishes and carted them off to The Bridge where, with the help of numerous volunteers, the kitchen soon was ready to function. At that point Sister Jo and I moved in, with Marlene and Barb joining us later.

Although we were not officially open, requests kept coming to accept runaways, but without a license we had to refuse these requests. The licensing bureau told us that we would receive a provisional license in a few days. Our final approval would depend on the fire marshal.

In November, believing that the provisional license was on its way, we started to accept runaways. When I returned after taking a day off for prayer and quiet, six girls had arrived.

The fellow from the licensing bureau called to tell us that he wasn't the one who could do the licensing and that a new man was assigned to us. It was December, we still had no license or funding, and by now 32 kids had stayed with us.

Two licensing inspectors finally showed up bringing with them the fire chief. Most of the place looked good to them; however, a fire alarm system had to be installed and three fire extinguishers purchased.

The health inspector was our next visitor. His contribution to the never-ending list of things to do was to tell us that we had to have a dishwasher and an over-the-stove charcoal absorber for odors. Talk about frustration! I asked the inspector if he thought all of these things were really necessary. He replied that he didn't think they were but it was his job to impart what the law said. I suggested to him, since he didn't agree with the laws he was trying to impart, he should quit his job and work toward making the law more reasonable.

Finally in February we got a temporary, one-month license, and on March 8, 1971, we were finally licensed as a group home. By that time a total of 186 kids had stayed with us.

Although The Bridge was going well, we sisters realized the place was much too hectic to be our only home, so we moved elsewhere. We also realized we had to increase our staff because ten or twelve kids were often at The Bridge, and so Sisters Rita McDonald and Mary Wagner joined us.

Because The Bridge had no dependable funding, we were behind on the rent by $1,200, but through the efforts of our lawyer, Dave Stanley, the rent was paid. His group, the Enablers, also agreed to send us $200 a month for a year. In addition to Dave's immense financial help, his legal expertise was crucial.

The board of directors of The Bridge wrestled with the question of whether or not the group home should become autonomous. My concern was its survival without the backing of Catholic Charities. I was in Florida visiting my sister, who was ill, when I received a phone call from Dave telling me that The Bridge's board of directors had decided to make it independent from Catholic Charities. Dave wanted to be sure that the name "The Bridge" was my invention. It was, and so it happened. The Bridge was now independent, free to make its own decisions, sink or swim.

But the group home needed funding, so I invited Betty Danielson, whom I had met through the Runaway Assistance Program, for lunch. During our meeting I updated her on the progress of The Bridge. She was so impressed that she returned the next day with other members of the committee, who unanimously agreed to back us and try to get us funding.

In the spring of 1972 the Minneapolis Star Tribune featured The Bridge in a long article in which the captain of the Minneapolis police force was quoted as saying that the police had had "good relations with The Bridge in the past year." I hoped that the article would also get us some funding.

The Bridge was functioning very well, so I went back full time to the Free Store. The store was busy, and donations were plentiful. I was delighted when a clothing drop box was donated, certain that the drop box would solve the problem of boxes and bags being left at the front door, because these items were ransacked constantly.

The drop box proved to be a mixed blessing. At times I would find someone sleeping in it, and occasionally it was used as a bathroom. Some people donated their garbage, including dirty baby diapers. Once I found a gunnysack of blue-eyed kittens that had survived amid the bags and boxes. Sometimes a person who had crawled inside threw the contents of the box on the sidewalk as he or she dug to the bottom. Of course, the lock on the box would have to be broken to do these innovative things. The drop box did provide a conversational piece for the neighborhood. Everybody was always telling me "who dun it." I often threatened to shut the Free Store down if that box was broken into one more time—but what good are useless threats?

When the Fall of 1972 came, the winos seemed to be imbibing more than usual. I drove Sonny, one of the regulars at the store, to the detox center. A few days earlier I had had to call an ambulance for Francis, and the street news was that Norman was in detox. This meant three of the regulars were now gone. I hoped they would remain where they were for the winter. But I must confess that I missed them.

Late one January afternoon I received a phone call from another helping organization telling me that a woman had to be moved by nightfall and needed a truck or trailer. I told them I couldn't help her at that late hour, but I would pay for the rental of a trailer for her. Later she called to tell me that Ryder Truck Rental, in north Minneapolis would rent her a trailer and that it would be okay if I paid them in the morning.

The next morning I went to pay the bill. I told the man it was good of him to trust her and me. He laughed and said. "Her story was so wild that it had to be true. She didn't know your full name, what order you belonged to, or what you looked like. I asked her if she was Catholic, and she said 'No, Lutheran.' It was all so mixed up that it had to be okay."

Small monetary donations kept coming to the store, checks for five dollars or ten dollars. A check for $15 came from a man in Rice Lake, Wisconsin, whose daughter had run away from home a year and a half earlier and who had gotten clothes at the Free Store. I was concerned, however, whether the store could remain open because we had no steady source of income.

What we did have, however, was a steady stream of customers, many of them elderly, like Ida and Amelia, who visited the store often. Ida lived alone in a little corner house just a block from the store. Quiet and reserved, she didn't trust people. She came to the store to look over the pots and pans section. Walking was not easy for her, and she often had rags tied around her feet and ankles. Slowly she came to trust me. The big breakthrough came when she let me into her house. Together we made decisions about what food could be tossed from the refrigerator. Everything that was green and shouldn't be green could go, plus food with various other kinds of growth. The numerous dishes on the floor with hardened cat food were scraped clean. Her legs and feet also got attention.

I was out of town when Ida died. I had not known she had relatives, but I heard that soon after she died several relatives had shown up to claim their inheritance. They didn't stay long.

Amelia lived in a high-rise across the street from the store. Badly crippled from arthritis, she used a wheelchair. Occasionally I visited her. I learned that she had never married and had no relatives. I knew of a family who wanted to "adopt" a grandmother, and so it was arranged that Amelia went to the Klug family on Christmas day. Amelia called me later to report that her Christmas was so wonderful that she could hardly believe it.

The Bridge in 2005.

I had now been "on the streets'" for five years and had received a crash course in the harsh realities of life. I learned that the street people are "us." We all share the common goal of wanting to be happy and loved, but these goals are impossible to reach if there isn't someone who cares if we get up in the morning or not. I felt the pain and anguish of parents looking for a runaway child and knew sadness at seeing a good mind blown away by drugs. I grieved over a fine young man who died of a drug overdose and whose body had been found under a bridge. Daily I saw the struggle to survive, but I also shared in lighter moments when wit, humor, and stories would create laughter and camaraderie.

I find it hard to put into words the depth of my feelings for the world that I had suddenly and unexpectedly become part of five years before. I became very comfortable with this world because of the acceptance and love I received from the street people.

But my Spirit was telling me it was time to move on. I needed more quiet and prayer time. The inner voice that sets my time schedule is like a pull or call that sends the salmon upstream in the spring and the robins south in the fall.

Do the salmon know that they will die? Do the robins know that they will return? Both go, answering some mysterious, ancient call that somehow I believe is also in me. I am both Martha and Mary of the Gospel story, a mix of action and contemplation, each clamoring for her time.

The timing of the Spirit calling me to more quiet and prayer couldn't have been better. My community had just sent out a notice asking for volunteers to start a house of prayer. I applied and was accepted to be one of the six core members.

4

House of Prayer
Time to Feed My Soul

The six of us began in February 1974 to search for a good location for the community House of Prayer where the sisters could come for days of silence or a week retreat. We checked out a lovely old house in Taylors Falls, Minnesota, and a former convent in Stillwater, Minnesota. I liked the Taylors Falls home even though it was old and in need of repairs. The split-level convent in Stillwater wasn't as "homey," but this building won out because of its location and the number of bedrooms. A thirty-minute drive from the Twin Cities, the convent was accessible by city bus.

Besides helping to make the House of Prayer ready for occupancy in July, I spent the next few months trying to wrap up things at the Free Store. In May I went to see the landlords about the rent problem. They were just drafting me a letter about withdrawing their support, but said that they would have another meeting about the issue. In the meantime Ruth Halverson, who was running the store, went up and down Cedar Avenue getting signatures in support of keeping the place open. When June came it was still open but behind on the rent.

My last day at the store was at the end of June. Several of my "non-street people" supporters hosted a spaghetti dinner in my honor. Their wild plans included giving me a trip to Switzerland, but I got their offer pared down to a set of tapes by Thomas Merton. I said farewell to my wonderful Cedar Avenue friends and turned my attention to answering my inner voice appealing for more prayer and silence.

In his book, *Care of the Soul*, Thomas Moore writes, "When you find tolerance in yourself for the competing demands of the soul, life becomes more complicated, but also more interesting.

An example might be the contrary needs of solitude and social life. In most of us there is both a spirit of community and a spirit of solitariness." My spirit of solitariness was asserting itself.

The six of us moved into the House of Prayer on July 1, 1974. There was little diversity in the group. Five had been teachers, four in grade school and one in college, while I had been a medical technologist. However, we did represent an interesting range of personalities and gifts, including cooking, gardening, and artistic abilities. Each of us had a sense of humor, a true blessing because, as I remember, not one of us could carry a tune. We had come together as community for silence and prayer.

Our day was balanced with communal prayer, private prayer, and silence. We shared the house chores, ate our meals together, and enjoyed our daily times of recreation. Once a week we had a "hermit day," a time of silence until the evening meal.

We had picked a good site for the House of Prayer. Stillwater is an incredibly beautiful old town. Huge turn-of-the-century houses perch on high hills overlooking the St. Croix River, which borders Minnesota and Wisconsin and runs between steep, rocky banks. In the evenings we walked those hills, and occasionally on a hot afternoon we swam in the river. We shared many meals in our backyard under a giant maple tree whose leaves turned brilliant in the fall.

The arrangement of the house and the small backyard lent themselves to peace and quiet. The chapel, at the juncture of the two wings, had a row of varied color windows high on the east wall letting the morning sun stream in. We removed a few pews in the chapel and provided large pillows to sit on.

We were fortunate that several sisters could create beauty out of arrangements of twigs, leaves, rocks, and weeds. Their arrangements, never massive bouquets, were simple and delicate, reminding me of beautiful Japanese art. A graceful arrangement of the strikingly beautiful pink tea roses from our back yard remained my favorite.

Sister Marie Phillip, the oldest member of our group, tended our small garden with loving care. Her garden activities attracted the neighborhood children, and soon we had lemonade and cookie afternoons.

Amid this beauty and quiet I celebrated my silver jubilee as a Sister of St. Joseph. Of course, the "silence" was considerably shattered as friends arrived to share a backyard picnic, swap stories, laugh, sing, and rejoice in the wonderful gift of friendship and community.

During my first months at the House of Prayer my mind was divided. Ruth Halverson, who was now running the Free Store, had raised some money from churches, but if it weren't enough to pay the rent, the store would have to close.

In retrospect, I believe it would have been better if the House of Prayer had been up and running before I joined the group. I now found myself straddling two commitments, the House of Prayer as well as the Free Store. The Bridge was doing very well, and the Free Store had good help, but there was no steady income to pay the rent.

On November 19, I received a call from Ruth's daughter telling me that her mother had died. Ruth had not been feeling well when she arrived home after work at the store and died in a cab on the way to the hospital. Her funeral was a sad day for all of us.

Other faithful volunteers came to help at the store. Sisters Laura Geyer and Kathy Niska worked one day a week. (Kathy, who had helped at the store four years earlier when she was a University student, was now a CSJ.) Then a great blessing occurred. Sisters Marguerite Corcoran and Rose Tillemans received one of those mysterious inner callings, and so the Free Store was blessed with two wonderful full-time workers.

Of course, money was still a problem, but before the end of the month a $2,000 check arrived from the O'Shaughnessy Foundation, via Larry O'Shaughnessy. This wonderful windfall relieved my anxiety over the rent problem for the store.

All of this activity was not what I had envisioned when I signed up for the House of Prayer. I did know, however, that life rarely is as one envisions it—and the unexpected twists and turns make life an exciting one-way ride.

With the arrival of two wonderful, responsible sisters to run the store and money enough to pay the rent for some time to come, I finally could settle down and focus on my need for quiet and prayer.

Seven months had already passed. My divided attention had plucked from me the precious time of quiet, so I signed up for another year at the House of Prayer. Slowly I adjusted to a less hectic life—but no less interesting. I had inner and outer landscapes to explore.

The beauty of the outer landscape with the changing seasons did much to feed my soul. William A. Quayle in his book In God's Out of Doors echoes my feelings: "I love trees all the year through—in spring when their coy green is hinted at rather than come; in summer when they make dense shadow...in autumn, when the summer greens are forgotten and trees are a sunset's splendor. I love this procession of changing charm and meaning, but confess of believing that winter trees are more beautiful to my eyes than those of spring, summer, or autumn."

I, too, favor winter trees. The beauty of bare trees on snow-covered hills silhouetted against an evening sunset always feeds my soul. Awakening to a world of trees and bushes covered with hoarfrost is for me a moment touching on ecstasy. Winter is my favorite season.

My inner landscape also had summer and winter times. On some days my insides soared with happiness, and on other days I wondered what caused that happiness. The slowing down and centering process took time. The plaque hanging on our kitchen wall read, "Don't just do something. Stand there." To "just stand there" took considerable practice. But I loved the silence, and gradually my prayer life became less distracted.

I treasured the time I had to read and think. I thought about time and the fact that all time is pure gift. I wasn't promised next week nor even the rest of the day. That reality remains with me to this day and enriches my life as I am conscious of how fragile life is. I wanted to live life to its fullest and be grateful for each day.

I became more acquainted with the Bible and resonated with the numerous passages that spoke of doing justice, paying just wages, rescuing the oppressed, and being mindful of the poor and the needy.

From the Second Book of Samuel, I learned that sometimes extraordinary means are required to get attention when the usual channels are ignored. When Absalom wanted to see the king, he summoned his servant Joab to send him to the king. Joab refused to come, even after Absalom summoned him a second time. Absalom then instructed his servants, "You see Joab's field that borders mine, on which he has barley? Go set it on fire." This got Joab's attention. He went to the king with Absalom's message (2 Samuel 14:28-32).

Like Absalom, I have learned that extraordinary means are at times necessary to get attention. Setting fires, however, I would not ascribe to. In the future I would get into enough trouble by merely stepping over a white line, but that, too, got attention.

In the Gospel of John a line that seldom gets much attention spoke volumes to me. Jesus says, "I tell you this that my joy may be yours and your joy may be complete" (John 15:11). I pondered that statement because I couldn't remember ever hearing a sermon on the joy of Jesus.

Part of the "joy of Jesus," I believe, is having friends. In November 1975, Sister Char Madigan, a friend of mine, came to the House of Prayer for prayer and quiet but also to talk. We discussed the possibility of starting a house of hospitality for women and children in the Catholic Worker tradition.

The Catholic Worker way of living—a combination of works of mercy and justice, simple living and prayer—attracted us.

Dorothy Day, co-founder of the Catholic Worker movement, was an inspiration to us. Both Char and I had been fortunate to have met Dorothy Day.

During a visit to my sister's home in New York State in 1967, my mother and I visited with Dorothy at Tivoli, the Catholic Worker farm. After we had lunch with Dorothy and the group of people staying at the farm, she gave me a copy of her book, St. Therese of Lisieux. In the front of the book she wrote, "Bless the Lord, O my soul: and all my being bless his holy name" (Ps. 103). When we were leaving, I asked Dorothy if I could take her picture. She said, "What do you want a picture of a tired old lady for?" I snapped her picture— and knew that the visit had been a privilege.

A photo of Dorothy Day that I took in 1967 when I visited her at Tivoli, the Catholic Worker Farm in New York State.

Char had spent the summer of 1975 at the Catholic Worker House in New York City. She returned with these words of Dorothy ringing in her ears and an urgency to do something about them: "There should be a house of hospitality in every parish. It makes good sense that it would be the convent."

Our discussions led to our decision to start a Catholic Worker house after I had completed my two years at the House of Prayer. And so the dream was born—to establish a house of hospitality for women and children in the inner city of Minneapolis.

Sister Laura, who had helped out at the Free Store, heard of our plans and asked to join us. When the three of us held a meeting at the St. Stephen's, an inner-city parish in Minneapolis, we seemed to be of one mind. We agreed that each of us would meet individually with Sister Miriam Joseph, our province director, to share our plans and dreams. When I met with her in January 1976, she was very supportive and encouraging.

With this dream of a house of hospitality floating around in my head, I still had six months left at the House of Prayer. "Well, Rita," I told myself, "Let it float around, don't try to catch it. Dreams will get anchored when the time is right."

After four months I called Char to see how things were going. She and Laura, after scouring the neighborhood around St. Stephen's for a house to rent, had found two that might be suitable. I joined them in Minneapolis to check out the houses. As we were reading the small print on a "For Rent " sign in front of a house, the owner suddenly appeared. He indicated that he was not usually around at that time but just happened by.

The building was a triplex. The second-floor four-bedroom apartment would soon be vacant and rent for $275 a month, including utilities. Of course, we had no money, but with the help of $700 a month from our CSJ community, we would take the place for a starter. Although the apartment was small, there was expansion space in the same building—or we could look for a larger house.

The building, located near the inner city parish of St. Stephen's, had at one time been surrounded by beautiful, large homes lived in by residents who could afford them. Those residents were now long gone, and numerous apartment buildings and nursing homes dotted the area. This shift in housing brought an increase in the multicultural and multiracial population of the area. St. Stephen's, now a poor parish, struggled to provide emergency services to the many people who had fallen through the safety net.

With our dream now more of a reality, I peacefully completed my two remaining months at the House of Prayer. My two years there, which had been a fruitful time in my life, confirmed my leaning towards solitude, silence, and prayer. However, my time at the House of Prayer had been much busier than I had imagined it would be. My own concerns about the Free Store and the future dream of a Catholic Worker House were part of my busyness. The other part was the purpose of the House of Prayer. Sisters came for days of prayer or a week's retreat, which added to our work: shopping, laundry, and cleaning. I kept thinking that someday I would head to a hermitage. I haven't made it there yet—but I'm still dreaming.

Being a firm believer in transition time, I took a week and went to the woods.

For more than 30 years I had gone to a favorite spot of mine, a log cabin belonging to my cousins Frank and George, located on Third Eagles Nest Lake near Ely, Minnesota, my mother's home town. Both in winter and summer I had stayed at the cabin. Each season had its own beauty.

This cabin, on Third Eagles Nest Lake near Ely, belonged to my cousins Frank and George. In summer and winter, the cabin was a haven to replenish my spirit.

Winter was special. The cabin had no running water and was heated by a giant furnace that devoured huge chunks of wood. The heat rose in the cabin through a register in the floor. There was no access to the furnace from the living area, so adding wood entailed a jaunt outside to the small door to the furnace room, where I bent a bit or bumped my head. When the furnace went out on winter nights, usually at 2 a.m. or 3 a.m, I'd slip on necessary clothing and step out into a moonlit winter wonderland. I loved the sound of crunching snow as I walked. On occasion I was treated to a magnificent display of northern lights. The greens, yellows, and blues danced high in the northern sky on those clear, cold nights amid trillions of stars. I never minded when the furnace went out.

My first time spear fishing produced a nice 10-pound northern. Mary Ellen Foster, CSJ, (holding a box of decoys) was in the ice house with me to witness all the excitement.

Sometimes I sat on a bucket and fished with a line. Lilly Long, CSJ, shoveled snow and chipped the hole in the ice.

That July I spent some time hiking and reading, but early in the mornings I fished. In the afternoons I often fished too, and when evening came—I fished. Having a line in the water always anchors me. For hours I could sit in a boat or on shore, and as long as I had a line in the water I was at peace. If I caught a fish, fine, and if not, the time thus spent was still precious. The silence and solitude brought me deep inner peace and joy.

When the time came to reel in my line and head back to the Twin Cities to help open a Catholic Worker house, I again entered an unquiet and turbulent world.

5

St. Joseph's House
The Catholic Worker Way

Our common dream/hope to try the Catholic Worker way—simple living, meetings for clarification of thought, and prayer—became a reality. After I returned from Ely to Minneapolis, I joined Char and Laura at the apartment we had located on Second Avenue South, which became our first Catholic Worker house. We unpacked donated kitchen articles, cleaned rooms, hung curtains, and arranged furniture. We organized our chores: Char would clean, I would shop, and Laura would keep the books. Both Laura and I would be responsible to keep the car running. Each of us would "take the house," that is, be responsible or in charge two days a week and alternate Sundays.

Our guests came from a variety of agencies: Chrysalis, a center for helping women, Hennepin County General Hospital, churches, the rape center, and Women's Advocates. Often the women who were referred to us were battered, suicidal, or depressed. A few were pregnant. We offered lodging, food, a nonjudgmental space, a listening ear, and safety. Helen, our first guest, came before we were officially open, and Julie, who lived across the street, came crying because her boyfriend had tried to strangle her.

From the very beginning of St. Joseph's House we kept a daily log. Whoever was in charge of the house that day

St. Joseph's House at 2101 Portland Avenue in Minneapolis is getting its third coat of paint—dark red. I think Char picked the color.

logged in all requests for housing, pertinent information about what was going on in the house, names of visitors, and any other bits of information she thought the next person on duty should know. To remember those years I have turned to these logs, now kept in Char's archive room next to her office. The archive room contains boxes of the history of St. Joseph's House. With amazement, a bit of nostalgia, and often with laughter, I recently relived this portion of my life.

One of the first log notes, written in big letters by Char read: "RITA, YOU MUST PRINT YOUR LOG ENTRIES. YOUR HANDWRITING IS ABOMINABLE." My handwriting has not improved with age.

Our Catholic Worker house had space problems from the beginning. Our two beds for guests were immediately filled. Our living room doubled as a room for visiting, reading, praying, meetings, naps, music, crafts, play, ironing, and meals. We had no time limit on our guests but, as Char put it, at times they would "stretch our compassion level." We would accept the women for the day they asked for, but they might still be with us three weeks later.

For our own mental health and the good of everyone living at the house, we needed a bigger place. We kept our eyes open and our collective ears to the ground.

Meanwhile my interest in the Free Store lingered on. I got a call that the Free Store had been broken into and a fire had destroyed part of it. When Char and I went to check it out, we found the back door burned black and the place a mess. Sister Marguerite had hung a sign on the front door, "Closed due to fire." I felt sad, but I hoped the store would somehow survive and reopen.

What is it that sets off a mean streak in people so that under the cover of night they burn, batter, or destroy? And when the dawn comes, do they ever feel shame, guilt, or remorse? Of course, it's better that they batter buildings than people.

Things do get balanced out. Often sad news is followed by good news. Good news for our Catholic Worker House arrived in the form of Joe Skelly. In addition to the three of us who opened the house, several people showed up regularly, giving us immense help. Joe was one of the pillars who became a large part of our lives for years. Joe's bent was philosophical, and, in keeping with the Catholic Worker tradition, he led us in many long discussions. Why do we do what we do? Should we be doing what we are doing, or in the manner that we are doing it? (Years later, we were still discussing these same questions.)

Three guests—Mavis, Vicky, and Ann—went in and out of our lives for years. All had numerous needs that challenged not only our patience but all other Christian virtues as well. But they became very dear to us. As their mood swings went up and down, we learned to wait out the dark times and welcome their lighter and funnier sides.

Early on, someone from Chrysalis called. A pregnant woman named Carol was leaving her abusive husband and needed housing immediately. We attempted to find alternative lodging for her where she would get more support for herself and the baby, but we were the only option that she would take. We agreed to accept her with stipulations. Char had Carol repeat back that Carol would care for her new baby, feeding, bathing, and diapering him. And so after Carol gave birth to little Jack, they both came to live with us.

Jack required more attention than most babies, but often Carol was asleep so others in the house met his needs. When he was barely a week old, after two days and nights of vomiting, he was admitted to the hospital and had surgery the next day. All went well, and three days later little Jack returned. The first months of his life he spent with us.

In the first four months that our house was open, 125 women and 60 children had stayed with us. Our need for a bigger house was urgent. Most women came because of fear of a man, mental anguish, or chemical dependency. Some, unable to pay their rent, had been evicted. Mavis, one of our perennial guests, returned to tell us that she was pregnant and that she was out of food. She also wanted us to find someone to clean her apartment!

Our search for a larger place led us to a fine old house located at 2101 Portland Avenue South in Minneapolis, only six blocks from our original location. The house had six bedrooms, space in the attic to expand, and a basement for storage. The big question was, "How was the property zoned?" The owner, Don, reported that zoning would allow five unrelated adults to live in the house. That was good news. We decided to buy the place at the agreed-upon price of $32,000 with interest at eight percent and payments of $250 a month. But, of course, we had no money.

Don called two months later saying that he was coming over for us to sign the contract for deed. He thought we would have the $10,000 down payment waiting for him, but we explained that we had understood that it was due the next month. All of this prompted Char to send out our first newsletter, our cry for help.

She wrote a short explanation of who we were, what we had gotten ourselves into, and what bigger things we were headed for. She wrote, and we mailed. The letter went to friends, relatives, and supporters asking them if they could pledge five or ten dollars a month for the daily running of the place, food, household expenses, maintenance, and utilities. They, the supporters, would be our answer to "how do you plan to sustain yourselves" question when we tried foundations for the $10,000 down payment.

Did we really think that we could jar loose $10,000 from any foundation in less than a month—or for that matter, ever? But a miracle did occur. In response to the letters almost a hundred people sent in checks for amounts ranging from five dollars to $1,380. Their generosity brought in more than $7,000. Don accepted $7,000 as a down payment with our assurance that he would receive the remainder in April when two south Minneapolis churches were giving us their Lenten Project contributions.

On March 2, 1977, we signed the papers, and the house was ours. We named it St. Joseph's House in honor of St. Joseph, the patron saint of the Sisters of St. Joseph.

We wrote in our next newsletter: "The why of all of this? The God of the Gospel is, of course, at the heart of the matter."

The cleaning of the new house on Portland now began. We swept and washed, heaved and hauled, painted and polished, scrubbed and scraped. We lined shelves, arranged furniture, and stacked dishes. Donations of bedding, towels, pots and pans found their place, as did some heart-warming green plants. The place and pace was hectic, but we finally got settled.

Our overwhelming gratitude for all of this activity went to the numerous people who put in hours of work to get the place spiffed up. Help arrived from our relatives and friends, Sisters of St. Joseph, the Catholic Alumni Association, students from Holy Angels Academy, and parishioners from St. Stephen's.

Almost immediately we had calls for housing: one from Hennepin County for a woman and a child and another from Catholic Charities for a single woman. We turned down those requests because we weren't yet open. Then came a call from Catholic Social Service in St. Paul looking for space for a sister from out of town who was pregnant, and so the first guest in our new home was a Catholic sister.

We hurriedly moved beds in, and on March 10, 1977, we slept in our clean, new home. By the end of the month we had six other women and a four-month-old baby living with us, and we were full. By the end of April we had some 40 requests for housing but could accept only 11 adults and three children. Mavis, our frequent guest/visitor, had had her baby.

Two other valuable workers joined us. Lucy Arimond, an attorney more interested in doing justice work than prosecuting, and Rosemary Raditz, who became part of our stable community, and moved into a small bedroom in our basement. Sister Laura, friend and companion since our beginning, left us to work with young adults at St. Stephen's parish, so we said fond farewell to her.

Donations of food were a blessing that helped greatly with our food bills. Our June food bill went down because we received five gallons of pumpkin ice cream, boxes of noodles and Wheaties, a big sack of onions, and some delicious "defective" pizza. Also, miracles did occur: a meat loaf meant to serve six lasted for the 12 who were at supper.

In the tradition of the Catholic Worker we had meetings on Friday nights. These meetings, announced in our newsletter, were open to the public. After a soup supper we had what Peter Maurin, co-founder of the Catholic Worker movement, called "clarification of thought." Peter's idea was, as he expressed it, "if I give you a piece of my mind and you give me a piece of your mind, then we both have more on our minds."

These evenings of sharing were meant to broaden our horizons, deepen our understanding of social issues, and move us to action. So weekly we had speakers on topics of tax resistance, redlining, nuclear waste, pollution, the arms race, Nestle's infant formula, and the Mexican farm workers' grape boycott. We heard about the dignity of work but also the degradation of the work of prostitution. We never lacked for speakers or topics for these challenging evenings.

By fall, 130 people had stayed with us, including 40 children. The stories of the women were heart-wrenching. If they did get enough courage to speak to a clergyman about abuse, the response often had been, "What did you do to provoke him?" or "Try harder to be a good wife." These women also faced the problem of where to go with two or three children and how to get there.

Calls for housing were constant, as were calls from two of our frequent guests. Mavis called because she was short of money. She had spent her last few dollars on a steak and bells for her shoes, and Vicky wanted to know how to fry chicken. I spent a good amount of time explaining to her what a frying pan looked like.

Two unannounced visitors to the house were city housing inspectors. They caused some anxiety and a bit of anger in us.

Their many ideas on how to improve the place would take money. We couldn't provide private rooms when we had a hundred requests a month for housing. And we were not running a boarding house. We were a sisters' residence, and the women staying with us were our guests. The inspectors left with nothing solved.

In the same month the inspectors visited us, the washing machine went off balance—but not unannounced. We discovered this problem when we heard the ironing board crash into the opposite wall as the machine went hiking across the floor, pushing everything in its path. It took four of us to get the washing machine back in place ready for its next run. The repairman said that its condition was incurable, so its hiking days were over and ours began, for we had to hike to the laundromat until we could invest in a new washer.

Before the snow came, several volunteers painted our garage door green. Two shiny new garbage cans, gift of a women's group at St. Helena's parish, stood next to a fence bordering our neighbors' yard. The neighbors had two huge dogs, a Great Dane and a German Shepherd, who leaped with bared teeth at any of us who approached the garbage cans. Only the bravest took the garbage out.

The housing inspectors came again. They wanted a hearing on the issue of our house. In the Fall of 1977, I went to their downtown meeting to recite my litany: "No, we are not a boarding house." "No, the women are not charged for staying with us. It is a convent, a private home. The women staying with us are our guests." "No, they are not permanent residents but guests staying with us for a short time." " No, it is not a boarding house. It is a private residence and the women staying with us are our guests. Sister Char and I live there. It is our only home." "No, we don't charge the women for staying with us. It is not a boarding house. It is a private home." The inspectors didn't know what to do with us or what to call us. The meeting was adjourned.

Char, in our Christmas newsletter, captured the essence of what we were all about. She wrote, "Christmas is forever changed for me. It is sadder now. Too often I have murmured, 'I am sorry, we have no room for you.' Yet, it is happier. Never before have I been privileged to say so often, 'Yes, we have room, come.' Yes, because of so many people who choose, month after month, to be Samaritans. Christmas here is every day. Each day we bow down in the stillness, catch our breath to realize that we do behold, we do be held by God."

We started off on a rare note the first day of 1978: the place seemed normal. Breakfast was in shifts. We had a nice beef dinner and popcorn by the fireplace in the evening.

With January's cold weather our fuel bills skyrocketed. Our philosopher and faithful worker Joseph Skelly froze his beard nailing plastic around our windows in minus 20 degree weather. Lesson learned: start nailing earlier.

Soon after occupying our house we had visions of expanding into the attic. The inspectors, of course, did not share our vision. On March 10, the day we celebrated our house's first birthday, we received a letter from the inspectors denying us permission to remodel the attic. We prayed and waited. Another letter arrived. The inspectors had changed their minds. A permit was granted allowing for three bedrooms in the attic; however, another inside stairway was required.

Before we could really savor the happiness of it all, along came another inspector. This one was concerned about food. He wanted to know how we stored it, where we stored it, and how clean the place was. He suggested numerous and expensive improvements. I explained to him that we certainly wanted a clean kitchen and well-prepared food but this was a convent, Char's and my only home, and we could neither afford, nor did we want, the equipment he suggested. We wanted to live simply in accord with the Gospel and with the people who were our neighbors and guests. The inspector left. No changes were forthcoming.

Spring arrived, and the plastic came off our windows. Tulips, iris, and rhubarb poked through the ground, and we were told that the attic renovations would cost $3,900. Meanwhile, Sally was in jail, Janet's water broke (she was in the hospital), the second floor bathroom was filled with smoke because of a cigarette butt in the wastebasket, and Mary was playing the guitar and singing Christmas carols.

We received a call from a social worker who informed us that Mavis, along with her baby who had been placed in foster care, was missing. We were asked to please return the baby to foster care if the two of them showed up. Four days later we received a call telling us where they were. Char went to do the retrieving. The baby's name, according to Mavis, had been changed from Autumn to Crystal.

A women's carpenter group came to do the attic job. They brought wood for the ceiling from a friend's dismantled green shed. They nailed the green side down and gave us a fine plain wood ceiling. This quiet attic space allowed for a small prayer room. But there was cost overrun on the attic. The original estimate in May of $3,900 had, by July, reached $7,000.

While the attic was being fixed, the house needed painting and the mouse holes in the house foundation needed plugging with steel wool and caulking. "May we no longer be a mouse sanctuary," said Char.

Our 13 beds continued to stay full as did our two couches. Affordable housing was hard to find, and our guests often spent long days apartment hunting. Ione, one of our guests, had walked the streets for three weeks with her seven-year- old son looking for an apartment. "Landlords," she said, "will take dogs but not kids."

At St. Joseph's House I learned the importance of "attitude adjustment." All my life I have hated stinky ashtrays. Although we did not permit smoking in the bedrooms at St. Joseph's, the first floor was loaded with ash trays, all in constant use. My crusade was to train the women to empty their ashtrays after smoking. Whenever I had four women trained, they all would be gone by the weekend. I started over on a new four, while working with those still in the house. Over and over this happened, and I was finding that my attention and energies were narrowing in on ashtrays.

"Rita," I said to myself, "it is time for an attitude adjustment. You are in a losing battle—you can't win this one." I paid no more attention to ashtrays.

In the month when we had 55 guests stay with us, our house plumbing went on the fritz. Simultaneously seven of us got the flu—the plumbing kind. It is hard to have an attitude adjustment with something like that.

Meanwhile, our attic progressed nicely, and we hoped soon to have the house painted. But our big need was to renovate the kitchen. A fellow I knew only slightly said that he would expand our kitchen for free by knocking out an outside wall that faced our back porch, thus enlarging our kitchen. This would give us more cupboard space and a nice, big window.

I should have known better. After roughing in an outside wall and tearing out the ceiling, half of the kitchen floor, heat ducts, and an inner wall, he disappeared for three months, and then permanently. So we were torn up, cold, and too far along to turn back. Again we were begging for funds, this time to cover my trust in this "nice man." Well, it certainly wasn't the first time that I had been "taken." It confirmed my belief that slick talkers cover a wide range of humanity.

Our kitchen finally got back into shape, and the house, at least on the inside, was presentable. Our living room became the place of the joyful wedding of Joseph Skelly and Laurie, two of our faithful workers. The house was filled with song, prayer, food, and laughter. And, in the fullness of time, Char and I were godparents for Michael Patrick Skelly.

While our house was being painted, the painters discovered that squirrels had eaten our roof to the tune of $4,100, and peace had not settled down on our house. One guest overdosed on aspirin, and another cut her wrists at 1 a.m. Money was taken from Char's billfold, and in the night our car had been whisked away by two of our guests.

How could a place like St. Joseph's House keep going? What sustained us and our work? Always, the four indispensable ingredients for running a place like St. Joseph's House were prayer, volunteers, money, and a sense of humor. Without humor I doubt if anyone would last long in a place such as St. Joseph's.

The whole reason for our existence was in response to the teachings of Jesus. Prayer was the foundation of our life, although it took different forms at different times. When we began St. Joseph's House, both Laura and I attended charismatic prayer meetings. Char was a bit blown away at times by our freedom of expression but was grateful and touched that we changed pronouns to avoid sexist language in the readings. Later I felt called to pray in other ways.

My contemplative spirit found refuge in our little prayer room on third floor. When a longer time was needed to replenish my spirit, I went to our House of Prayer in Stillwater, Minnesota.

Through the ups and downs of St. Joseph's House, I was sustained by my belief in what Gamaliel told the court in Acts 5:37-38: "If their purpose or activity is of human origins, it will destroy itself. If, on the other hand, it comes from God, you will not be able to destroy them without fighting God himself."

Without volunteers and money, St. Joseph's House would have ceased to exist. Month after month and year after year hundreds of people faithfully sent in their donations, often accompanied by a touching note explaining why they did it.

Numerous volunteers contributed countless hours. They came from diverse parts of the city, stayed for varying lengths of time, and brought a variety of skills, unique personalities, humor and laughter. Our helpers were men and women, young and old, of different races and religious beliefs.

One of them, a dear friend of mine, Sister Rose Alma Wojick, a cancer survivor of some 18 years, came regularly to help with our mailings. At one of our Friday night meetings, she spoke of her thoughts on death and dying. Her positive attitude towards life was summed up by her statement, "No, I am not afraid to die. I only have infinite curiosity."

After she died, among her belongings I found these words written on a piece of scrap paper: "To be a contemplative is to be free to love. This requires a great deal of unselfishness and total detachment from all things. To be free to love is to be free to die—to leave all things unfinished and go to God without regretting the interruption." That is exactly what my dear friend Rose Alma did.

Spring reminds us of resurrection and nature was reawakening. Not everyone, however, was pleased with the reawakening of all nature in the Spring of 1979. Char noted that mice and cockroaches were coming out of hibernation. "Curses," she said, "I am for war, while Rita of Assisi smiles."

Besides the calls for housing we occasionally had odd requests. When Laurie, a volunteer, answered the phone one day she listened intently and then she asked the caller to repeat her request. The lady caller had told her that she felt she was possessed by a real and active demon. She wanted Rita (me) to perform an exorcism. A former guest of ours had told her that "Rita did that sort of thing all the time." What could I do but laugh?

In October 1979, we had a Halloween party to which guests and former guests were invited. We asked them to come in costume. Ann, now out of the psychiatric ward and living alone, arrived in blue jeans and a sweatshirt. "Ann," I said, "remember, I told you that this is a costume party."

"I am in costume," she said, "I came as a nun."

One cold January day the doorbell rang. Two big men in dark suits stood there. My alarm button went off because they were obviously not from the neighborhood. They produced badges identifying themselves as CIA agents who were looking for Charlotte Madigan and Rita Steinhagen. The two of us were curious as to what big crime they were tracking down. We learned they had received a call from a Linda, at our address, who told them that Char and I were planning to blow up the Panama Canal. Staggering news! What an ambitious project. But quite beyond our expertise—or interest.

We explained to them who Linda was. She spent much of her time either behind her bed or under it, making a tent-like structure with sheets that she lighted with various colored lights. When spices were missing from the kitchen, we could usually trace them to her tent, where she mixed exotic concoctions. We told the agents that they had just seen her, for as we had opened the door to let them in, she was going out to put one of our young guest's salamander in the snow. The agents left, and neither of us, as far as we know, have had the CIA looking for us again.

I would so like to tell the stories of all of the women and children who came to stay with us—more than 600 by the end of 1979. Their stories are repeated over and over in the lives of the poor and marginalized; nevertheless, each woman was unique. I learned that being beaten by an enraged, drunken husband is not reserved for the poor alone. If the husband is a doctor, lawyer, or CEO of a large corporation, the humiliation and scandal of the beatings often keep the wife silent.

If I were to pick one word to describe the women I came to know, it would be "tired." They were tired of standing in line at the welfare office only to be told that they were in the wrong line, or wrong building, or given the wrong forms and told to come back tomorrow. Tired of bundling up their kids to take them every place they had to go, whether the grocery store, laundromat, appointment, or house hunting. Tired of waiting for buses in the cold with children who were cold and hungry. Tired of waiting for the landlord to fix broken toilets and outlets that didn't work, to repair cracked windows and doors that did not shut properly, and to exterminate the ever-present cock-roaches and mice. Tired of being evicted for asking the landlord to fix such problems. Tired of being told "no kids allowed." Tired of having boy friends or husbands harassing them—and worse. Tired of carrying bags of dirty laundry to the laundromat three blocks away. Tired of selling their bodies to pay the rent. Tired of being called "those people" without ever being spoken to civilly by the people who use that phrase. Tired of lying that their bruises and black eyes were from falling down stairs. Tired of being tired. The list could go on.

And I was tired too. I had begun to divide my time between working and living at St. Joseph's House and taking care of my mother. She had lived alone in a small town in southern Minnesota after my father's death in 1974, but had been finding it hard to get around and keep up the house. We made the deci-sion to move her to Minneapolis and I found her a two-bedroom apartment a mile from St. Joseph's House.

One weekend when I was out of town, I got a call telling me that she had fallen. She had broken no bones, but the doctor said that she needed more care and supervision. So after five and a half years I left St. Joseph's House and moved into my mother's apartment. I was blessed by having a mother who was easy to live with. She was never demanding and had a good sense of humor. It was a sad day when her care required her to move to the First Christian Residence, a nursing home, which luckily was in the same area as her apartment.

Leaving St. Joseph's house was not easy for me. This dear place has burrowed deep within me and left memories of a diverse group of people with all of their sadness, joy, pain, laughter, jokes, heartaches, disappointments and, yes, at times, resurrection. My years there were an unforgettable time in my life.

While living with my mother, I took a less stressful job work-ing at the Dorothy Day Center in St. Paul, which was run by Catholic Charities. In December 1981 the housing situation for the street people was critical. Mary Hall, a former nursing residence owned by St. Joseph's Hospital, was across the street from the center. I called Dolore Rochon, CSJ, the hospital administrator, to ask her if there was empty space in the building. To her affirmative reply, I invited her for coffee at the Dorothy Day Center to talk about the possibility of using Mary Hall for housing.

She was very sympathetic to the idea and, in record time, she handled the negotiations for renting the second floor of Mary Hall to Catholic Charities. A call went out to our sisters for help in staffing Mary Hall. Twenty-five sisters showed up for a one-evening training session. The next night, New Year's Eve, two sisters welcomed four women to Mary Hall.

At first open only to women, the shelter accepted men within a week and remained open from January to April 1982, the time agreed upon for the rental. The men's wing was full every night with a nightly waiting list of 30, and the women's wing was nearly full most of the time.

Although I liked my work at the Dorothy Day Center, I preferred the freedom of not working for a large organization such as Catholic Charities. I decided to join Lynn, who was starting The Mustard Seed, a storefront where we distributed food, personal items, and clothing. As is always the case, we had the continual problem of raising funds for rent, as well as a stipend for us and for one of the street people we hired.

The next two years were very difficult for me. The house where I was living with other sisters was sold. Twice I moved before joining two sisters of my community living in a small home on Laurel Avenue in St. Paul. The month I moved there, one of them, Sister Mary, was diagnosed with cancer. A week later, during a terrible blizzard, I drove my mother to the hospital for eye surgery. Spring brought the news that my brother David, who was living in California, was seriously ill, and my brother-in-law Bob had cancer.

After a visit to David in June, I went alone to my favorite refuge, my cousins' cabin near Ely. The beauty, silence, and solitude of the week did much to feed my soul and lift my spirits to face the hard days ahead.

My mother was admitted to St. Mary's Hospital in September 1983. When she died a few days later, my feelings of sadness and loss overwhelmed me. I now grieved two great losses, my beloved mother and St. Joseph's House. I felt a deep sadness for both losses, and I knew I would face more losses. David and Bob were both seriously ill, and Sister Mary's cancer had progressed.

In October I wrote in my journal: "Friday was a hard day, I didn't go to work. I stayed home and went through Mom's things, the little bit that she had."

It was the "little things" that got to me. I found a snap clothespin that she had used in the nursing home to pin her napkin to her dress. She had written on it, in very shaky letters, "Ruth S." I very slowly took strands of hair from her hair brush. All of her belongings fit in two paper bags. She had given away everything she possibly could. When she had nothing left to give, she saved her paper napkins for me to take home. I cried a lot on that Friday, remembering the little things.

My dear brother David died the following January, and April took my brother-in-law. Both funerals were very hard. By the end of the year the Spirit was telling me it was time to move on. I needed to broaden my horizons.

6

Texas
Learning Spanish "Puedo"

For some time I had been interested in learning Spanish and had tried half-heartedly to teach it to myself. The number of Spanish-speaking people in the Twin Cities had increased greatly in recent years, so I decided that now was a good time to get serious about learning the language.

Somewhere I had picked up a brochure about a Spanish language school located in El Paso, Texas, so in January 1985 I left for Texas to study Spanish.

The small brochure advertising Liceo Sylvan, the language school I attended, said the students would be be living with a Mexican family in El Paso. My Mexican family turned out to be Quica, a small, 82-year-old-woman who lived alone in a former grocery store. The building had a small kitchen and storage area, a bathroom, and a larger room that served as our living room, dining room, and bedroom. Although Quica spoke no English, her eyes spoke volumes, and we got along just great. On occasion we played cards in the evening using Quica's Mexican deck, the likes of which I had never seen. We played, despite my not knowing what on earth I was doing, and occasionally I won. Her response was always the same, "Oh sheeet."

One day Quica was trying to tell me something, and I could not understand what she was saying. I did understand, however, when she said, "You study all the time and you don't know nothing."

I replied, "Quica, you have lived in the United States all of your life, and you don't speak English. How do you expect me to learn Spanish in three weeks?" No answer.

Liceo Sylvan was eight blocks from her home on the other side of a dozen railroad tracks and occupied the second floor of an old school building that had heating problems. Our teachers were Mexican women from the neighborhood who spoke little or no English.

It was from one of the students, Father Larry Rosenbaugh, that I first heard about the School of the Americas (SOA), a U.S. Army combat training school located at Fort Benning, Georgia. Latin American soldiers who trained there were responsible for the deaths of thousands of human rights activists, students, religious leaders, union members, and peasants. Soon after I met Father Larry he was notified to report to the LaTuna prison north of El Paso. He and Father Roy Bourgeois had received prison sentences for climbing a tree near the barracks of Latin American soldiers on the Fort Benning base and playing the last sermon of Archbishop Oscar Romero, the Archbishop of El Salvador, who was shot dead while saying Mass March 24, 1980. In his last sermon Romero had demanded the soldiers lay down their arms and quit killing their fellow countrymen. Two of the three officers cited for his murder were trained at the SOA.

After four months of language study, I stayed on in El Paso and volunteered at Annunciation House, a shelter for refugees from Central America. Annunciation House, an old building and former convent, is located ten blocks from the Rio Grande River that runs between El Paso and Juarez, Mexico.

In the late 1970s, Annunciation House had become a shelter for the homeless. Originally anyone who knocked on the door had been accepted, but eventually the staff had decided to receive guests only from

Annunciation House, a big, old former convent, has been a safe haven for thousands of refugees fleeing civil wars in their country.

Central America. When conflicts had arisen in the house between United States citizens and non-English speaking persons, occasionally the U.S. citizens would report the others to the INS. The staff decided that U.S citizens had other options.

Lunch hour at Annunciation House.

The last remaining member of the original five Americans who had started Annunciation House was Ruben Garcia, who is still there today providing hospitality, challenging the system, and running a tight ship. I learned a lot from Ruben about kindness, justice, and commitment.

The vast majority of those who came to Annunciation House had fled their countries because of civil wars. Most came from El Salvador and Guatemala, countries where the U.S. was supporting cruel and corrupt military regimes.

The journey to the U.S. for all who arrived at our door had been horrendous. Just getting out of El Salvador and Guatemala was life threatening, and the long trek through Mexico was, more often than not, very inhospitable.

Guests at Annunciation House often tried to make contact with a relative or friend who was living in the U.S. in hopes of making their way to them. Leaving El Paso, however, was a major problem, always risky and often dangerous. Immigration officers stationed at the bus depot, airport, and the checkpoints on the only two roads leaving El Paso made the chances of getting north very slim.

The clothing room in the basement of Annunciation House played a vital role in the traveling plans of those hoping to leave. I would help them select dark clothes if they were leaving at night to hop a train. If they were going by bus or airplane, I would have them dress like a college student in jeans and tennis shoes with a backpack. At times this worked, sometimes it didn't.

Train hopping was very dangerous and sometimes resulted in injuries. More often than not, early the next morning, we would find the person who had left sitting by our door with a discouraging story to tell. Legal help was available to the guests who were applying for asylum, but it was a long process. Those guests would be at Annunciation House for many months.

Sixty to 70 people often stayed at Annunciation House. Two dormitories on the first floor housed the men, and a dormitory for single women and small private rooms for families were located on second floor. Occasionally on a Saturday night we piled

Getting ready for a Saturday night dance at Annunciation House. The fellows were excellent dancers.

the dining room tables and chairs in the kitchen and a boombox blared wonderful Central American music. I danced with excellent dancers until midnight, the ending time according to house rules.

Volunteers, like myself, who staffed Annunciation House came from many parts of the United States, and one came from England. Our commitment varied from a few months to a year or more. Each volunteer was required to have a working knowledge of Spanish and was responsible for a certain number of guests. We were to keep updated on the guests assigned to us as to their plans for moving on.

All guests were assigned various house tasks and required to attend a mandatory house meeting once a week. Ruben led the meetings and read the names of each guest to make sure all were present. My Spanish would never win a prize, but occasionally I conducted the house meetings when Ruben was gone.

One Sunday morning I drove nine people to Mass at St. Patrick's Church. As I pulled into the parking lot, four green immigration vans surrounded our van. We were all taken to the immigration headquarters. Sister Lilly Long, CSJ, was also in the van and hauled off with us.

When they asked where I was taking them, I said, "To church." "They aren't dressed for church," they said. I replied, "Well, that's where we were and that's where we were going."

After we were photographed and fingerprinted, most of us were released, but two people were taken to the corralon, an immigration detention center. Later on one individual, who had just arrived at Annunciation House, was deported to Colombia. I felt bad about that.

Besides taking our turn as "guest servant"—a job that entailed answering the phone, greeting new guests, assigning them to a volunteer, dealing with any emergencies, and seeing that the meals were prepared and served—each volunteer had one assigned, ongoing task.

For many months my task was to be in charge of the pantry. I purchased the 100-pound sacks of beans and rice and 25-pound boxes of lard from the warehouse across the railroad tracks. In cooking the beans, the cook of the day would send someone to me with an empty two-pound coffee can and want it filled with lard to put in the beans. I would argue that one, but I usually lost.

Weekly I made rounds in the van to the numerous warehouses in the area to gather crates of unsellable fruits and vegetables. The guests liked to go with me because it gave them an outing and sometimes a piece of good fruit. On returning we would separate the useable produce from the questionable and those items past redemption.

At times the cockroaches in the pantry were a problem. One day they were really out of control; the pantry was black with them. And then there surfaced from deep in my brain a remedy advocated by Dorothy Day that I had read about years ago: boric acid. I purchased five pounds of the white powder and spooned it on the back of all of the shelves. The next day I was ready to canonize Dorothy when I saw that the shelves were no longer black and moving.

On my day off from Annunciation House and my pantry duties, I often walked the neighborhood, usually to the wonderful Bowie Bakery, but at times I went to the river that runs between Juarez, Mexico, and the U.S. Most of the guests at Annunciation House came through Mexico and crossed this river from Juarez. In this area the river is not very deep nor very wide, and its banks are now cemented into place to prevent flooding.

Many Mexicans crossed the river every day to work in El Paso as maids, janitors, or as yard or restaurant workers. Not having the proper papers to enter the U.S. legally, they crossed the river in various ways. Once I saw a woman being carried over on a man's shoulders. Some were pulled across on makeshift rafts or inner tubes. Others waded across when the river was low.

Early one Sunday morning I went to the riverbank and sat with a group of 20 or more people who had just crossed and were sitting against the tall fence that ran for miles on the U.S. side. They were watching for the migra (immigration) vans that constantly patrolled the border area and roamed the streets. When they could no longer see a van they made a run for it, hoping to disappear between the small houses or commercial buildings about a block away. Those caught were taken to the corralon and processed. If they were Mexican, they were driven to a distant bridge and released back to Mexico. They would then have to start the process all over again—and be late for work. If the person caught was

Crossing the river to El Paso.

from a country other than Mexico, they were kept at the corralon and waited weeks or months until immigration decided their fate.

This crossing process has now slowed considerably because taller and longer fences have been built, more immigration officers have been hired, and more vans, cameras, and lights are in use.

During my time at Annunciation House I also did laboratory work at a clinic on the outer edge of Juarez. Every second Tuesday I joined other medical personnel from El Paso for a bumpy ride in the back of an old van to the clinic perched on a hill among other barren dirt hills. These trips gave me a glimpse of the grinding poverty in which most of the world lives.

I am standing with my helper, Diane, in the clinic. I taught her how to do hemoglobins. Diane went on to become a nurse.

Soon after we crossed the river into Juarez, we would drive down the cement embankment to one of the main roads in the barrio. Giant potholes, old tires, bags of garbage, and numerous unrecognizable objects were common sights. Water from

Thousands of these homes surround the clinic (upper right).

an unidentified source often poured from a pipe onto the road. On either side of the road, sprawled upward on the bare hills, were hundreds of hovels constructed from packing crates, plastic, and pallets. Old tires or rocks held the roofs down.

People on their way to work stood along the way waiting for the bus. I have never seen whiter blouses or shirts. I pondered about the amount of work it took to have those white clothes. Because their houses have no running water, the people usually washed their clothes outside in tubs of cold water and strung the laundry to dry on fences in the sun. I expect that the hot sun acts as a bleach. Besides pondering on the whiteness of clothes, I pondered on the injustices of life.

Slowly we wound our way through the barrio and up the hill to the clinic and a food distribution center. The rule of Father Thomas, who started the food project years ago, was that every-one must work before receiving food. The men made bricks out of clay and straw and dried them in the sun. Women, holding four corners of a blanket piled with gravel, filled potholes on the road. Other women went to wash clothes for those who were ill.

One day I went with four of the women to wash clothes for a sick, elderly woman. We washed and rinsed the clothes by hand in huge tubs of cold water, then hung the clothes to dry on a barbed wire fence. We had carried the water in buckets from the common water pipe a block away. A small enclosure in the woman's yard held a couple of pigs. Nearby was an outhouse. I found the whole scene depressing.

Meanwhile the older people sat and prayed quietly in an open porch area near the clinic building. What was their prayer? What was going on in their heads? I wish that I had talked to them about it. I wonder what my prayer would be if I had been born and lived my life on those hot, windy, barren dirt hills.

At one o'clock all of the workers returned to the main building for lunch of beans, rice, and tortillas. Afterward I helped distribute the food to the people who had worked: beans, chili, potatoes, and onions. As the people were leaving, a man and woman knelt on the ground to pick up individual beans that had fallen in the dirt. Another woman and I knelt to help them gather the beans.

From the hill where I was gathering those individual beans, I could see the tall buildings of El Paso, a city built in the land of plenty—a land that wastes enough food daily to feed all the people of Juarcz and all the people in the surrounding hills and far beyond. Again I pondered the injustices of life.

On one of my days at the clinic, a woman named Jovita, who was nine months pregnant and ready to deliver, came to the clinic. The doctor asked me to drive her to the midwife. We climbed in the van and down the hill and over the bumpy roads we went. I tried hard to avoid the big potholes while she held her big stomach and gave me directions to her home. She wanted to stop to pick up her husband. He crawled into the back of the van. The first midwife's place was full so on to the next midwife we went. The baby was born shortly after we arrived.

At a Palm Sunday Mass, I became the madrina (godmother) for two beautiful little girls, Luz, whom I'm holding, and Maria de Jesus, who is being held by her father. Jovita, the girls' mother, sits to my right.

Five months later I was asked to be the madrina (godmother) for Jovita's baby. A big honor. Mary Wakefield, a nurse at the clinic, went with me to Jovita's home. When we arrived, Jovita said, "The other one too." The two-year-old hadn't been baptized yet, so at a Palm Sunday Mass in a beautiful church service, I became the madrina for two beautiful little girls: Luz, the baby, and Maria de Jesus, the two year old.

When an earthquake hit Mexico City in September 1985, I had another opportunity to use my laboratory training. The

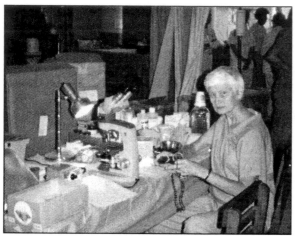

The makeshift lab in Mexico City after the 1985 earthquake. Lab work was minimal.

Salvation Army asked for medical personnel to go to Mexico City, so I flew down with the El Paso group. We left from the Juarez airport at night in the middle of a thunderstorm (which scared the daylights out of me) and arrived in Mexico City a little after midnight. The person who met us at the airport told us to use the bathrooms in the airport because the water in the building where we would be staying was being rationed. The common bathroom in the Salvation Army building where I stayed had signs that read "Flush toilets only early morning and late evening."

The doctors saw about 200 patients a day, most of them suffering from PQS (postquake shock). Many couldn't sleep or eat and felt as if they were falling. Others were dizzy and had diarrhea. The lab work I had to do was minimal, consisting mainly of urinalysis and blood counts.

We worked in one of the poorest areas of the city and hardest hit by the quake. Tents sent by the U.S., Canada, and the Red

Makeshift tents gave shelter to the earthquake victims. This one tent served 55 people. Nighttime visits from rats were a problem.

Cross created "tent cities" that sprang up in the middle of the street and on sidewalks. Other shelters consisted of plastic, cardboard, old blankets, and wood scraps. Three of us were invited into a shelter made of plastic that was about the size of a small living room where 11 families were staying, a total of 55 people. The tent had only a few pieces of cardboard, a badly mangled sofa, and a few old blankets. A woman told us that at night the rats tried to come in.

I was surprised not to see any large areas that were completely destroyed. Individual buildings collapsed next to buildings with no damage. Sometimes just the top floor of a building was gone.

The saddest sight for me was Hospital Juarez, an 11-story structure in the middle of a medical complex. It was the only building destroyed in the complex. The earthquake had happened on the day of the doctors' staff meeting at the hospital, and about 900 people died when the building collapsed.

The workers were digging on the ground floor of the hospital when we arrived.

Digging in the remains of Hospital Juarez that was destroyed in the earthquake. The building collapsed during a doctors' staff meeting. Nine hundred people died.

Relatives of those still missing in the rubble were camped in tents outside the fence surrounding the area. Behind one of the medical buildings wooden coffins were piled ready to be used when other victims were found.

Because we were hospital personnel in our scrub gowns, we were allowed in the closed-off area near the evacuation site. We also were given permission to enter the makeshift morgue in a nearby building, but I saw no reason to do so.

It was a hard week. Several volunteers returned to El Paso with respiratory infections because of the terrible pollution in Mexico City. I had a bad cough for the next two weeks. We all returned with sad memories.

Back at Annunciation House a nudge from the Spirit told me it was time to move on. I had listened to the stories of the guests in the house for two years. They had sparked my interest in Central America, and I wanted to experience for myself the reality of their lives.

A volunteer at the house told me about an organization called Witness for Peace, which had members stationed in Nicaragua. I applied to the group and was accepted, contingent on my fluency in Spanish.

To improve my Spanish I lived for six weeks with two Immaculate Heart of Mary sisters from Michigan who were working in an extremely poor barrio in Juarez. Although my knowledge of a Mexican barrio increased, my Spanish still lagged, so I applied to a language school in Antigua, Guatemala and traveled there in 1987.

At one time the capital of Guatemala, Antigua was a well known tourist attraction. Its numerous large churches, destroyed by an earthquake and mud slides in 1773, had never been rebuilt. The rubble and walls, tunnels, and inner rooms of these magnificent structures left me in awe.

Antigua had more than two dozen language schools in operation. Often these "schools" were no more than a room, opened by some enterprising person who saw the great number of students descending upon Antigua to learn Spanish now that Guatemala was deemed "safe" for travel. The war against Guatemala's peasant population by the military, which had raged for years, had now subsided.

I learned about this tragic history when I had picked up a book at school whose brown paper cover obscured its title, I Rigoberta Menchu, an Indian Woman in Guatemala. After reading the book I understood the reason for the brown paper cover.

Rigoberta, a Maya Indian, was from the El Quiche province of northern Guatemala, where the massacre of thousands of peasants had taken place less than ten years before. The army personnel responsible for this slaughter had never been brought to trial. This genocide destroyed Rigoberta's family and community. Her book, written in 1983, powerfully told her story and touched me deeply.

(Later I was to learn that the SOA had played a key role in the training of the Guatemalan military leaders who conducted the genocide against the Mayan civilian population. This scorched-earth policy of kidnapping, torture, and murder left 200,000 dead during Guatemala's 36-year civil war. A human rights report released by the Guatemala Archdiocese Human Rights Office in 1998 linked the SOA to a civilian-targeted genocide campaign. Soon after the release of that report, Archbishop Juan Gerardi, of the Human Rights Office, was brutally murdered. A year later, in March 1999, U.S. president Bill Clinton acknowledged our country's role in Guatemala's civil war and admitted that our support of right-wing governments during Guatemala's civil war was wrong.)

At school I had an excellent teacher, Letty. We often discussed a wide range of issues—but never their civil war. Married for 12 years, she had two children. She told me that her husband, who worked in Guatemala City, had never been home for supper in all their married life. After work he went to his mother's

I'm with friends in the park in Antiqua, Guatemala. Don't miss the basket on the head of the girl to my left. Since she has been big enough to walk, she has been practicing to balance a basket on her head.

home in Antigua to eat supper with her and his unmarried brother who lived with her. I asked Letty if she would like him home for supper. When she answered in the affirmative, I told her to ask/tell him to come home to eat with his family. She did—and he did.

Guatemalans love parades, kites, balloons, and firecrackers. They have the custom of setting off firecrackers at the door of a person having a birthday. This activity takes place at dawn before the cock crows. I was amazed at how many people who lived near me had birthdays.

The hot air balloons delighted me. These large, colorful balloons made of special paper were launched from the top of a stepladder on festival days. When a wad of rags, soaked in lighter fluid and fastened to the opening of the balloon, was ignited, these beautiful, multicolored balloons soared slowly upward and out until they disappeared in the night sky.

Guatemalans have another unique custom. During Mass, at the elevation of host and chalice, a man outside of the main entrance lights a small bomb the size of a baseball. The first time I heard the explosion, I stood bolt upright, thinking we were being attacked. The gentle smiles of the Guatemalans next to me assured me that we weren't.

My days in Antigua passed quickly and peacefully, but one day I witnessed a tense situation. A large crowd of men and women had gathered in front of the government building. Soldiers with rifles were standing at the edge of the crowd. I asked someone what was going on and was told that the night before, soldiers in trucks had gone through the town and picked up all of the young men they could find to be in the army. The parents of the missing boys were trying to find out where their sons were.

Soldiers with guns are standing at the edge of a large crowd in front of a government building. The previous night, military personnel had snatched many young men in the town to force them into military service. The parents of the missing boys are trying to find out where their sons were.

Halfway through my studies in Antigua I received a call that my sister had fallen and broken several bones. She was a widow with no children, so I returned to the U.S. and stayed with her for several months before returning to Guatemala in February 1988.

When I returned, I was extremely tired, had no energy, and had developed a terrible cough that lasted weeks. I had just started to feel better when I got fleas and diarrhea and was violently ill for a night. Things like that made studying a challenge.

When I felt better, another student and I went to Chichicastenango, a village perched on a mountain summit that is famous for its huge mercado (marketplace). We were packed 60 in a bus that was built for 40. It is hard to get rid of fleas with such togetherness. We traveled up a beautiful, winding mountain road for three and a half hours to get to Chichicastenago.

In this village the large white church sits majestically next to the marketplace. In the main aisle of the church, three or four box-like structures contained sand where people placed gifts of

When you ask for long-stemmed lilies at the *mercado*, this is what you get! I shared them with Sister Georgiana who came from Guatemala City to celebrate St. Joseph's Day with me.

flowers, fruit, vegetables, and occasionally a small flask of rum, along with candles to be burnt for the dead.

On March 19, the Feast of St. Joseph, Sister Georgiana, a Sister of St. Joseph from California who worked on the outskirts of Guatemala City, came to Antigua to celebrate the day with me. I shared with her the long-stem lilies I had purchased from the mercado in Antigua.

Easter came early in 1988, so I was fortunate to be able to participate in the elaborate and moving Holy Week services before I had to leave for Nicaragua. In preparation for Holy Week the people spend days making alfombras (rugs) in the middle of the streets. Most of the rugs were made from colored sawdust but occasionally from flower petals. The colors and patterns of these rugs are often as intricate as those of Persian rugs.

The processions, with incense bearers creating huge clouds of smoke, started on Palm Sunday and continued all week. Throngs of people packed the narrow cobblestone streets. All day and into the night the processions continued. When it was dark, a glass coffin containing a figure of Jesus was carried through the winding streets. A light in the coffin illuminated His reclining figure.

The main religious celebration was held on Good Friday. The people can identify with the suffering Jesus, but the resurrection and Easter Sunday are not as meaningful to them. I was surprised to see a half-empty church on Easter Sunday.

During the four months I was in Guatemala, I came to love the people and the country, a country torn by a long civil war that will take years to heal. At dawn I boarded a plane to fly to Nicaragua. There I would join Witness for Peace and encounter another country torn by war.

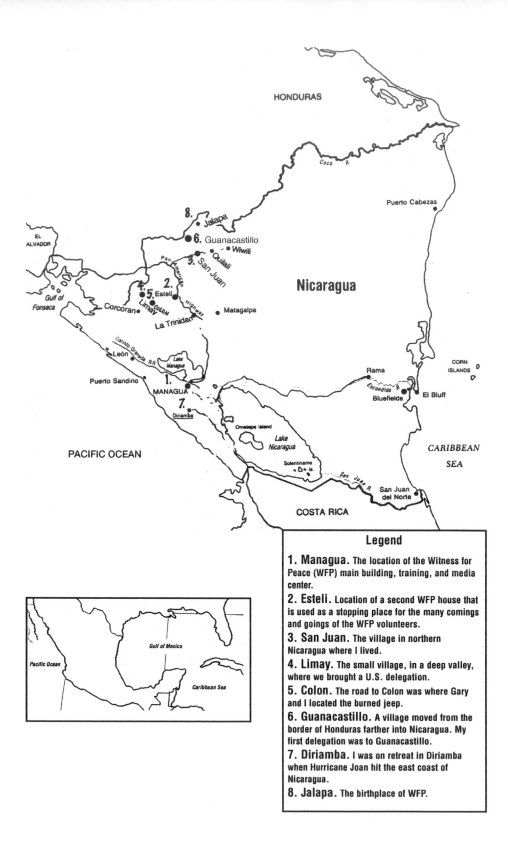

HONDURAS

Coco R.

Puerto Cabezas

EL ALVADOR

8. Jalapa

6. Guanacastillo
Wiwili

3. San Juan
Quilali

Nicaragua

Gulf of Fonseca

4. 5. Esteli 2.
Limay COLON
Corcoran
La Trinidad

Pan American Highway

Matagalpa

Corinto-Grande RR

León

Lake Managua

Puerto Sandino

1.
MANAGUA

7.
Diriamba

Rama

Escondida R.

Bluefields

El Bluff

CORN ISLANDS

PACIFIC OCEAN

Ometepe Island

Lake Nicaragua

Solentiname Is.

San Juan R.

San Juan del Norte

CARIBBEAN SEA

COSTA RICA

Gulf of Mexico

Pacific Ocean

Caribbean Sea

Legend

1. Managua. The location of the Witness for Peace (WFP) main building, training, and media center.

2. Esteli. Location of a second WFP house that is used as a stopping place for the many comings and goings of the WFP volunteers.

3. San Juan. The village in northern Nicaragua where I lived.

4. Limay. The small village, in a deep valley, where we brought a U.S. delegation.

5. Colon. The road to Colon was where Gary and I located the burned jeep.

6. Guanacastillo. A village moved from the border of Honduras farther into Nicaragua. My first delegation was to Guanacastillo.

7. Diriamba. I was on retreat in Diriamba when Hurricane Joan hit the east coast of Nicaragua.

8. Jalapa. The birthplace of WFP.

Nicaragua
"What if I should be killed tomorrow?"

My eight months as a volunteer with Witness for Peace (WFP) had a profound influence on my life. Although I had lived in poor areas and had seen grinding poverty, nothing I had experienced could compare to Nicaragua in 1988, where the people always feared for their lives. Working in a clinic, or school, riding public transportation, or working in the fields was dangerous. I learned that no one in Nicaragua was safe.

A brief history. In 1912 a peasant named Caesar Augusto Sandino led a popular uprising against the presence of the United States Marines, who had occupied Nicaragua for 20 years. The Marines were recalled in 1933, but not before they had trained and armed the native Nicaraguan National Guard and set up Antonio Somosa as the commander.

The Somosa family, backed by the U.S., had ruled Nicaragua for 50 years and by 1975 had amassed holdings in more than 500 corporations, including newspaper, television, and radio stations.

In 1979 a group of revolutionaries calling themselves Sandinistas (in honor of Sandino) overthrew the Somosa regime. Before fleeing to Honduras, the National Guard, following Somosa's orders, massacred civilians, destroyed crops and factories, and bombed schools and hospitals.

During the 1980s remnants of Somosa's National Guard, the Contras (counterrevolutionaries), now based in Honduras and funded by the U.S., conducted a violent struggle to regain power in Nicaragua.

In 1983 a group of religious activists from the U.S. had visited Jalapa, a small farming community near the Honduran border that was frequently being shelled by the Contras. They noted that the shelling stopped when U.S. citizens were present.

These activists launched the organization Witness for Peace to try to address the problem of safety for the Nicaraguan people. They invited U.S. citizens to live in the war zones in Nicaragua, hoping their presence would deter the shelling of any villages where they were living. The organizers knew theirs was a crazy idea, but it generated a quick and generous response. In April 1988 I was one of eight new volunteers who arrived in Managua to join WFP as long-term team members.

In Managua we underwent an intensive two-week training program that included a history of WFP, an update on the situation in Nicaragua, training in nonviolence, and information on the different regions of Nicaragua. We met with people on both sides of the conflict, pro-Contra and pro-Sandinista.

As WFP volunteers we would live in the war zones, document Contra attacks on civilians, host delegations from the U.S., and act as a deterrent to the shelling of the villages where we lived.

During our training our proficiency in Spanish was evaluated. I was not surprised to be told that I was one of the four who needed to improve our Spanish by living with families in Managua for a month.

Before the four of us went to live with these families, we attended the monthly WFP team meeting held in Managua for the long-term volunteers. These 30 volunteers came to share their stories about living in the small villages in Nicaragua's war zones. They spoke of villages that had been attacked by Contras and the funerals they had attended. They told us of land mines, shellings, rockets, kidnaping, fleas, parasites, scabies, lice, malaria, and diarrhea. They described these conditions as being simple facts of life in Nicaragua.

Their stories brought to life for me the meaning of the words of Father Miguel D'Escoto, minister of foreign relations of Nicaragua, written in large letters on the wall of our meeting room:

I came to see the cross was the greatest act of love.

It was the total gift of love; you not only give your goods, you give your life itself.

And it's the greatest act of life—it's the act where
life is most manifest.

Therefore the cross is life.

And here my meditation began to consider that life
can't be measured in the number of days an existence lasts, but by the depth of commitment.

I pondered that last line in light of the fact that most of the volunteers were young.

After the meeting I went to live with a family of four in Managua. The father, a night watchman, went to medical school in the mornings; Chilo, his wife, helped out at a community center. They had two daughters, ages six and eleven. I slept on a cot in the one main room of their house, a square cinderblock building. The hot sun beating down all day on the corrugated metal roof did not make the nights conducive to sleep nor the days to study. At times I shared the small, dirt-packed backyard with a chicken tied by one leg to a piece of metal. I sat next to wet clothes hanging on a barbed wire line. There I tried to study Spanish and read.

I read Robert McAfee Brown's Unexpected News: Reading the Bible with Third World Eyes, in which he says: "To our third world friends, the Messianic event—will not just be a spiritual realignment of eternal values but a starkly political and social reversal." This book helped me to realize how political Mary's song, The Magnificat, is, especially the lines, "He has deposed the mighty from their thrones and raised the lowly to high places. The hungry he has given every good thing, while the rich he has sent empty away" (Luke 1:52-53).

Later, when I attended prayer meetings in northern Nicaragua, I realized the people read scripture with an understanding of their

import in their daily lives. They were looking forward to the ful-
fillment of these lines from Luke.

In all of the heat, Chilo's sister and her three daughters came
to visit. They only stayed overnight and left by 4:30 a.m. the next
day, BUT they brought two live chickens with them. Now when I
sat to study in the dirt-packed back yard, I had three chickens
running around me plus the sight and smell of garbage.

When not studying, I wandered the neighborhood getting to
know the neighbors. On Tuesday mornings I picketed at the U.S.
Embassy with other U.S. citizens living in Managua. The high
walls, coils of razor wire, and armed guards surrounding the
embassy made a strong statement that not all Nicaraguans were
pleased with the U.S. support of the Contras.

Ben Linder, an engineer from the U.S., had been killed by
the Contras in 1987 while building a small hydroelectric plant to
provide power to a remote village in northern Nicaragua. On
the first anniversary of his death, his mother and brother joined
us picketing at the embassy. After a short memorial service that
included songs, readings, and statements by his family, the group
boarded the bus for the two-hour ride to Matagalpa, where Ben
is buried. Just after sundown we walked in a solemn and sad
candlelight procession to his grave.

On that beautiful moonlight night, I walked up a hill in the
cemetery to look down on that peaceful, candlelight gathering
by Ben's grave. Thinking I was alone, I was startled to hear a
woman's voice beside me say, "We are standing on my son's
grave." When I apologized, she said, "Oh no, it is all right."

She told me that she had lost three sons and her husband in
the Contra war. She was now a widow who lived near the cemetery. I told her that our group was there not only for Ben Linder
but for all the Nicaraguan people who had been killed and
wounded in the war.

I was very moved by her story and couldn't imagine the pain
and sorrow of that woman, and the hundreds of Nicaraguan

widows with similar stories, largely because of a war funded by the U.S. government.

I found a wonderful, strong spirit in the Nicaraguan people. The poor in the barrio where I was living in Managua favored the revolution. The letters FSLN (Sandinista National Liberation Front) were painted in red and black on many buildings and posts. My neighbors explained to me that red is for the blood that was shed and black symbolized the grief and suffering of the people. They didn't want revenge but the right to be free to govern themselves. That seemed to me to be a very reasonable desire and not one to be killed for.

As part of my language training, I left Managua to go to Jalapa, the village bordering Honduras where WFP had been started. Sister Julie Marciacq, CSJ, who lived in Jalapa and taught physics, chemistry, and mathematics to high school kids, had invited me. She arranged for me to live with a family with five children. I shared a small room in a shed-like structure in the back of the house with their 18-year-old daughter and two cats.

The furnishings of the main living area in the house were sparse. Pictures, hung close to the ceiling, were of Jesus and the family's son who was killed in action. A larger frame held several more pictures, including one of their 15-year-old daughter in her casket.

Carlos, their youngest child, age three, was delightful. He usually ran around naked. Every morning he greeted me with his hands together in front of him and a bow from the waist. What a way for me to start the day—he was a joy to behold.

Although the family had a sink in the back yard, it seldom had water because the water pumps in town were broken and no parts were available from the U.S. This lack of water was hard on me. In the ten days I was in Jalapa, three times I walked a mile and a half to the river with the neighborhood women to wash clothes and bathe. I complained a bit that by the time we returned home we were again hot and dirty.

I was in Jalapa to upgrade my Spanish so the more conversations I had with the people, the better. Therefore one Saturday I walked with five women to the neighboring town of Carbon in search of food. We left at 7:15 a.m. and returned at 3:30 p.m. This walk about did me in. One woman wanted to buy duck eggs, the others beans and rice. No duck eggs or rice were to be found, but one woman purchased some beans at a farm.

In addition to Spanish, I also was learning the harsh reality of life in Nicaragua, where eight hours of walking in search of food produced such meager results.

Of the many people who touched my life in Jalapa, Rosa remains a favorite. She was an elderly woman living at the edge of town. I really don't know how old she was, but her sweet, wrinkled face made me think that she was older than my 60 years. Daily she walked past where I was living on her way to the jail to see her only son, who was imprisoned there. Because families had to feed the prisoners, three times a day she brought him tortillas and coffee. She would hand the food to the guard who took it to her son; then she would sit to wait for the empty plate and cup.

I often visited Rosa in her very small, poor shack. When I was leaving Jalapa, I went to say goodbye to her. She looked around her tiny kitchen for something to give me. Then she reached up, and putting her hand into a small kettle hanging on the wall, she handed me an egg. I was torn about what to do. I thanked her for her wonderful gift but explained that I was leaving that day and would have no place to cook the egg. I told her that a great gift to me would be her smile and would she walk with me a little way as I was leaving. She smiled at me, and, putting her arm around my waist, we walked together.

Back in the Managua office I met with Sharon to ask about my next step on the way to joining WFP. I asked her when I would have my next Spanish test, and she told me to sit down. We talked for a while in Spanish, and then she asked me where in Nicaragua I wanted to work.

"You mean that I am accepted into WFP?" I asked, to which she replied, "Of course."

As a long-term team member with WFP, I was assigned to the little town of San Juan de Rio Coco, Region 1, in northern Nicaragua.

My companion in hitchhiking from Managua to San Juan was Paddy Lane, a won-

Main Street, San Juan de Rio Coco, Nicaragua. Women and girls, with containers of corn on their heads, lined up by the door of the molino (mill) to have the corn ground. I lived two doors down from the molino.

derful woman from Alaska. Because her time with WFP was coming to an end, she would be introducing me to San Juan, where she had been stationed. We hitched a ride first to the town of Esteli, about half way to San Juan.

We were always hitching rides on anything that was moving because the bus service was very unreliable. When the bus did run, never on time, people were sitting on top of it and hanging out the doors and windows. Traveling by bus was my least favorite way to travel. Public transport trucks, with an open back and an overhead pipe to hang on to, also were overcrowded, but at least I could be outside where the air was fresher. My favorite mode of transportation was on the back of a pickup truck where I could sit on my backpack and survey the countryside.

In Esteli we stayed at the WFP house used by the volunteers in their many comings and goings throughout the country. Paddy gave me a short tour of the town, pointing out numerous bullet holes in many of the buildings, a sad reminder of the battles fought there early in the revolution.

The next day, in a gentle rain, we walked to visit Justina, a former nun who had worked with the Sandinistas during the revolution. Her passion now was to help the three groups in the Catholic Church to reunite: the base communities, the popular Church and the traditional Church. I wished her luck!

When Justina heard that I would be stationed in San Juan, she told us that it was caliente (hot). I thought at first that she meant the weather, but she meant the war.

When we returned to the WFP house, the electricity was out, so we ate our bread and a can of sardines in the dark. In the morning, with no food in the house, Paddy went to get some bread while I made coffee. After breakfast and morning reflection, an hour of quiet and sharing that we both looked forward to, we went to try our luck at hitching a ride to San Juan. After a three and a half hour wait, we got a ride in the back of a pickup truck as far as Condega. Three soldiers had climbed on the truck when we did. We never accepted rides on military vehicles and also tried to avoid riding on the same transport with soldiers. Occasionally, however, it was hard to avoid this.

We stayed the night in Condega and early in the morning caught a ride on a truck going to Polaquina. At the edge of the town, near a little steam, we waited for a ride to San Juan. Thank goodness we had a pleasant place to wait, because we waited for nine hours with no luck. A woman who had passed us in the morning and saw us still standing there when she returned invited us to her sister's house, which was just up the hill. We gladly accepted because we were tired and hungry. We ate tortillas and beans with gratitude.

Early in the morning we caught a local transport loaded with people, bags, boxes, and chickens. Two and a half hours later we finally arrived in San Juan dirty, tired, and hungry. The water in town was shut down so Paddy and I stayed hot and dirty.

We shared a room at the pension (hotel) with two other women, a man, and many mice. By evening I was feeling lousy, with a headache, body ache, and diarrhea. The next day I was really sick, and Paddy asked a woman she knew if I could stay with her. I was grateful to move to Hortensia's house. Hortensia is a widow who lived, with her flea-bitten little dog and scrawny cat, on the main road in town. I was terribly ill for two days but did rise on the third day.

When Paddy saw that I was going to live, she returned to Managua on the 5 a.m. public transport, which left at 1 p.m. She squeezed on the truck with 20 others and disappeared down the dusty, winding road. I was on my own.

As Paddy disappeared from sight, the reality of her leaving hit me. I was in a strange village in northern Nicaragua, the only gringa (white woman) and the only person with white hair for many miles. And I was still half sick. I had been sent to San Juan to get to know the people, to keep my eyes and ears open, especially as to what the Contras were doing, and to report what might be newsworthy to our communications center in Managua.

"Well," I said to myself, "Rita, get on with it!"

I continued to live at Hortensia's, spending my days walking the streets, checking at the mayor's office as to any Contra activity in the area, and visiting the people. Some families had sons fighting with the Contras, others with the Sandinistas. The pictures of family members who had "died for their country" were hung close to the ceiling in their homes. I found the town hard to live in because I could feel the tension in the people.

Hortensia's friend, Ronald, a pastor of an evangelical church, came to visit soon after I arrived. He warned me to be careful because the Sandinistas might shoot me and blame it on the Contras. "That's what they did with Ben Linder," he said. He told me that most of the people in town were Contra sympathizers so the town would probably be left alone. That suited me just fine.

While living with Hortensia, I prepared my own meals. Although I was feeling better, I found it a challenge to figure out what to eat. I hadn't been able to face a bean or rice when I was sick but I was ready to try again. So occasionally I would go to

Hiking the hills of Guatemala.

Elsie's cafe where beans and rice were the only thing on the menu.

Elsie, pro-Sandinista, had a son who was in the Sandinista army and was stationed in the area. At times he would roar around town in a jeep with his buddies, then stop at Elsie's. Standing their guns in a corner while they ate and drank, they would soon roar off again.

Elsie's was also the place where occasionally I would have a beer. By our special arrangement she would never set the bottle before me but would pour the beer into a large, metal cup that she brought to the table as she took my order for beans and rice. She would smile and wink as she set the cup down. I liked Elsie.

Across the street from where I lived there was a little fruit and vegetable stand run by Horatio and Francisco. At times onions or tomatoes were available (and a few vegetables unknown to me) but never bananas, although they were grown in the area. Huge trucks piled high with green bananas regularly went past on their way to Esteli or Managua.

When Francisco was called to the army, Horatio and I went to visit him. He was stationed not far from San Juan on top of a hill so high it was named Las Nubes (the clouds). After an hour's walk up the steep, winding road we came to the top. From one of the trenches Francisco hollered for us to come up. So we climbed higher to the numerous trenches and shelters built by the Sandinistas.

A half hour later we wound our way down the dirt road viewing miles of lush green countryside, blue sky, and white billowy clouds—so beautiful and so unsafe.

The next day Hortensia went to visit her relatives for four days, and I was left alone to guard the house and feed the flea-bitten little dog and scrawny cat. I itched all over. The little dog scratched constantly, and so did I.

Fortunately I was feeling better a few days later when Eric, another WFP volunteer, arrived to help arrange talks and housing for a WFP delegation from Kentucky that would be coming to San Juan. Eric was stationed in Wiwili, the second little village down the road beyond San Juan. That area was so dangerous that the public transport would not go beyond San Juan.

In addition to lining up homes where the delegation could stay, we arranged for them to hear from organizations on both sides of the conflict—workers in health care, education, agriculture, and government. When all was arranged, Eric and I hitched a ride on top of a load of green bananas and went to Managua to meet the delegation, and we returned to San Juan with them in the large vehicle owned by WFP.

After two days in San Juan we took the group to Guanacastillo, a resettlement camp about 15 miles north of San Juan. The people in this northern village had been moved farther into Nicaragua by the Sandinistas because the Contras just over the border in Honduras had been using their farms as a source of food and supplies.

Two pickup trucks took us to Guanacastillo. Riding in the back I had a panoramic view of the beautiful countryside and rolling hills. It all looked so peaceful, but I was aware that at any moment we could be ambushed or drive over a land mine that could blow us to bits. I never saw a farmer in his field without a gun leaning against the fence.

We arrived at Guanacastillo feeling very tired. That night we all slept on the floor of the building where the children were fed twice a day while their mothers worked in the fields. We had rice and beans for breakfast for those who were up to it and then had reflection time before the group left for the coffee hills where the women, using machetes, cut underbrush from the coffee plants. The community leader went with the group to explain the growing and processing of coffee.

I stayed behind to boil drinking water because the water in the village was so dirty it had plugged our water purifying pumps. The following day we returned to Managua with the delegation.

While we were in Managua, our media office asked Gary and me to investigate the death of a government man who had been killed west of Esteli. Gary Martinez, who had joined WFP when I did and was often my companion, would meet me the next day in Esteli. I left that evening with Carrie, a young woman from Canada who was working on a water purifying system with a group of fellow Canadians.

We left Managua at dusk and encountered an obstacle course the likes of which I had never seen in my life. Cars with tail lights or headlights out (sometimes both) would appear unexpectedly. Trucks, buses, carts, and bikes suddenly loomed dangerously close. People and animals walking on either side of the road and sometimes in the middle challenged Carrie's driving. Giant pot-holes were unavoidable.

Later that night Carrie dropped me at the WFP house in Esteli. The next morning Gary and I went to the government office to inquire about the their worker who had been killed. We were told that a government jeep had been ambushed one kilometer north of a co-op on the way from the small village of Colon. Two people had been killed outright and the third, Miguel, the government worker, had been struck on the head so many times that he was unrecognizable.

Our media office wanted us to find the jeep and talk to anyone who might know anything about the incident. I was scared. Knowing that I would be going into very dangerous Contra territory, I asked myself, "Why am I doing this?"

For the first time I felt the terror that the Nicaraguan people had lived with for years. The Contras were armed by U.S. tax dollars. My country was the major contributor to the terrible suffering of these people. I experienced fear before while traveling other roads, but on this assignment my fear was intense. I pondered the situation. For the first time I was really feeling what it was like to live with the daily reality that one's village, home, or family could be attacked at any time, day or night. There was scarcely a family in Nicaragua who hadn't lost a family member or relative in the war.

After many miles of walking, two campesinos arrive tired in San Juan. Their rifles are behind the man sitting on the table.

I found myself asking, "What if I should be killed tomorrow?"

First of all, I would be sorry for my sister Lois. We are the only two left of our family and have taken such different paths all our lives, she, a Florida sunbather, and, I, a Minnesota fisherwoman. She supported Reagan, and I strongly opposed his policies, but my friends would not need an explanation of why I went to Nicaragua. They knew me, loved and supported me. I was so grateful to all of them who were part of my life.

In spite of my fear, Gary and I went to the road exiting town and waited for a ride. After a couple of hours an ambulance stopped for us. The look of utter terror on the face of the ambulance driver told me that my fears were not unfounded. We climbed in the back of the ambulance next to several other passengers, and after the driver put two big white flags on both front fenders, we took off.

Gary asked the driver to let us off at the road going to Colon. I certainly would have missed this road, which looked more like a wide cow path with many mud holes and ruts. We started down the path, skirting corn fields, wading a knee-high river, and jumping mud holes in hopes of finding the burnt-out jeep.

Two women who got off the ambulance when we did told us not to keep going in the direction of Colon because it was muy peligroso (very dangerous). They took a different path, but Gary and I continued on. All was lush overgrowth and, for me, very eerie, with no sounds and no one in sight. We walked for quite some time on the marshy trail, wading the shallow, winding river several times.

When we came to a wider spot in the river, I said to Gary, "Nuts, I'm tired of wading rivers. Let's go back." Just then we saw a house in the woods to the right. Gary said, "Let's check it out."

We came to a small farm but didn't see or hear anyone. Again, I thought it was eerie. Finally a man appeared. We explained that we were looking for a jeep that had been burnt. The man was not friendly but he did give us directions. We crossed a field, waded another part of the river, then heard voices behind us. Two young women and a boy of about ten were following us. The women, carrying machetes, weren't friendly.

We soon came in sight of the jeep, burnt to an orange rust color. While I took several pictures of the jeep, Gary examined the license plates, some spent shells and part of a gun he found on the ground. One of the women asked me to help her find something in the woods. Not understanding what she was looking for, I declined her request. The place gave me bad vibes.

Three people had been murdered in this vehicle. One was Miguel, a government worker. He was the third son in his family to be killed in the Contra war.

The three people who had followed us soon disappeared. Gary and I walked back to the junction where the ambulance had let us off. After walking for two hours, we caught a ride to Concordia to talk with the family of Miguel, the government worker who had been brutally murdered in the jeep. His father told us that Miguel was the third son he had lost in the war.

We stayed overnight with Miguel's family. My sleeping quarters reminded me of a chicken coop without the chicken droppings. The room had a hard-packed dirt floor and a low, gray, weathered wood bench that was my bed. The place was clean, private, and silent so what more could I want? Gary stayed elsewhere. The cost for lodging for the two of us was less than a dollar.

At breakfast we were entertained by a parrot trained by Miguel's father to say a few words and to cackle like a chicken. The bird gave us a lighter moment amid the harsh reality.

Later in the morning Gary and I hitched a ride back to the Colon junction and retraced our steps. We were searching for Carlos, the leader of the cooperative who, according to Miguel's father, had heard the blast, seen the flames, and gone to investigate. When we found Carlos, he explained how he and his friends had found the bodies in the jeep and then had notified the authorities. With our heads and small notebooks full of the information we had gathered, we hitched a ride back to Managua to give our report to our media center.

I then returned to San Juan, only to find Hortensia, her family and friends, busy building a shrine to Our Lady in the room where I had slept previously. On this anniversary of the death of Hortensia's husband, they were decorating with flowers, pictures, and candles.

My sleeping quarters now transformed to a shrine, I went down the street to stay with Leonore, who had invited me to sleep at her place when I needed to. Leonore and her husband Pedro had a small tiendita (store) in the front part of the building where they lived. The pictures of their three sons, all dead, hung close to the ceiling in the store.

Juanita, the woman who worked for Leonore and Pedro, told me that Leonore, an alcoholic, had been drunk the night before and had been in bed all day. Juanita, her young daughter Isabella, and I slept in separate rooms in the storage area on the second floor. The goings on of the second night I would never want repeated.

At 8 p.m. I was propped up in bed reading. About 8:30 p.m. the racket started. Rats. Rats in the boxes along the wall, rats in the boxes and baskets at the foot of my bed, rats on the rafters above my bed. While my light was still on, the first two rats appeared, perched on an inside wall beyond the foot of my bed. They sat staring at me with their red eyes, then sauntered out of sight.

When I turned the light out to sleep, the racket started again. Rats in the boxes to my right and at the foot of my bed. On with the flashlight. Nothing in sight. Off with the light. More racket. It sounded like one of them fell. On with the light. Two of them running on the rafter over my bed. And so it continued for three hours. I counted 11 rats before I finally fell asleep—only to be awakened at 4 a.m. by more racket and another rat racing above me over my bed. I saw a dozen red-eyed rats that night.

By morning I probably had red eyes, too. I was grateful when the sun came up and I could drag my tired body back to Hortensia's house, where there were no rats and the cat kept the mice away. I had had a glimpse of another reality that I had never before experienced or thought about. In the warmer countries families often have their little stores attached to their living quarters. Those stores are often lined up one after another down the street with no solid partitions or ceilings. The stores become an inviting feeding spot for rodents. And I suspect that the situation is impossible to control.

Back at Hortensia's house the electricity was off. When the lights came on five days later, I went to the mayor's office to see about news of Contra activity in the area. I spoke with Myra, the mayor's secretary. She had no news but asked me if I wanted to go with her and Serio, a worker with the food distribution service, to Guanacastillo to deliver food for the children's program.

The Toyota truck we would be riding in had been ambushed a few weeks earlier. The driver had been killed, there were bullet holes in the vehicle, and the shot-out windshield had not been replaced. Nevertheless, we all went back to beautiful Guanacastillo with its kind people and beautiful children. On our return trip to San Juan it poured rain, and with no windshield in the truck we arrived sopping wet but safe.

It was especially dangerous to travel roads during or after a rain because the wires to blow up a vehicle were often strung through the mud puddles. Even in dry weather traveling the roads was dangerous. I shared the fear that the Nicaraguan people felt daily. I, too, would be glad when the war was over, but at any time I could return to the United States, the land of abundance, and leave behind a country so devastated that it has not recovered to this day.

It was time to attend another WFP team meeting. The only vehicle leaving San Juan was an ambulance that already had bullet holes in it. Because it was late in the day, I hoped they would wait until morning; however, they were ready to leave so I crawled in the back of the ambulance next to a fellow the driver said had tuberculosis. Off we went through the night with our red lights flashing.

Once in Managua I joined other WFP long-term team members and left for our meeting at a retreat center in Diriamba, a village 30 miles south of Managua. The volunteers were a fine group of young adults, but I did miss people my own age. Don Irish, a retired professor from Hamline University in St. Paul, Minnesota, was the only other person over 60. We rarely saw each other, however, because we were living in different regions of Nicaragua.

After the team meetings Gary and I were assigned to host another U.S. delegation, this one to Limay. I liked Limay, a quiet little town off the beaten path, settled in a deep valley, a two and a half hour drive over a rough dirt road from Esteli. The village had experienced much suffering in late 1984 and the early part of 1985. In a one-month period, 35 people had been brutally murdered on the roads near Limay. In one day 11 people had been killed in ambushes of various vehicles on the road to Esteli.

After arranging for sleeping quarters, Gary and I left Limay to check out a grape/wine co-op where we wanted to take the delegation. Juletta, a WFP member and a native Nicaraguan, drove the WFP Toyota to the co-op. The road was a river bed, or rather a river because the water was at least a foot deep and filled with big rocks. As I sat in the back of the truck that plowed through water, drove over huge rocks, sank in and out of giant muddy potholes, my admiration for Toyota pickup trucks was sealed. We hoped that the weather would be dry by the time the delegation arrived.

The next day in Limay, Gary and I had planned to locate families where the group could stay and to line up organizations to speak to them. However, the rain continued all night and all the next day, washing out the bridge to Esteli. The streets and fields were flooded, crops were lost, and families had to be evacuated. A couple of days later after the weather finally cleared, Gary and I, with the help of a community leader and a minister, lined up seven families where the delegation could stay.

Our task was now finished, but with the bridge out we were stranded. On a gray, windy day I went to the comedor (cafe) on the corner of main street, stood in the doorway, sipped sweet black coffee, and watched the town activities. Women and young girls walked by with plastic bowls of corn on their heads. A huge cow sauntered into the intersection. Young kids were selling tamales, the baskets balanced on their heads. A man hurried past carrying in his hand a fresh piece of meat that he had just purchased at an open air meat booth.

Two days later the transportation problem was solved, and we left Limay for Esteli. We were jammed together, standing in the back of a truck along with boxes, bags, chickens, and food to sell at the market. It was one helluva ride for two and a half hours uphill to Esteli.

I said to Gary, "I have had it. I'm not doing this any more."

Gary said, "This is what it means to stand with the people."

I replied, "Well, if I wasn't here, they would have more room to stand."

By the time the delegation arrived, Limay had dried out, and we were able to take the group to the experimental wine farm and to a tobacco co-op. The miles of pink and blue morning glories called *Santos de Dios* (Saints of God), climbing the bushes in the countryside with abandon, were the treat of the hour-long ride to the farms.

Both places we visited were desperately poor. The daily grind of trying to eke out a living was evident in the weather-worn faces of the men. Before we left, a man stood up and said, "What hope can you give us?"

Being from the country that has footed the bill for an aggressive war against them for years—and no change of policy in sight—what hope could we give them? That question haunts me to this day, for conditions have not improved for the people of Nicaragua.

We returned with the group to Managua, and, despite the threat of a hurricane, the delegation flew home as a new group of volunteers arrived from the U.S. The radio announced a hurricane would hit Managua the following afternoon. I was scheduled to make a retreat in Diriamba, so I hitched a ride to the retreat center and arrived to find that I was the only retreatant. The place had been full the day before with sisters from the Atlantic Coast, but they had returned home because of the hurricane threat.

I slept soundly and didn't hear the two huge trees that fell by the house. It rained most of the next day. When the sky cleared,

I went for a walk and bought a newspaper which showed pictures and reported the terrible devastation caused by Hurricane Joan on the Atlantic coast—across Nicaragua to the east from the retreat center.

Hurricane Joan's fury and force were incredible. Corn Island and the cities of Bluefields and Rama were wiped out. Another 20 to 30 villages were washed away. In addition to the human casualties, thousands of acres of crops had been destroyed, countless trees uprooted, and cattle drowned. The water was contaminated by insecticides and latrines. The hurricane left behind deep mud, downed wires, and twisted buildings. The poor were now more destitute than before.

I can't ever remember being so deeply affected as I was by reading about the massive destruction from Hurricane Joan. The sadness of this tragedy settled deep in my soul, and I wrestled with God over the age-old problem of pain and suffering.

I struggled with the lines of scripture, "Come to me, all you who labor and are burdened, and I will give you rest. Take my yoke upon you and learn from me and you will find rest for your souls, for my yoke is easy and my burden light." I saw no light burden for the people of Nicaragua, and I heard no answer from God to lift my spirits.

Eventually the sun came out. Still on retreat, I had days to ponder the overwhelming sadness of the Nicaraguan people, who have suffered years of destruction—of crops, electrical lines, bridges, and clinics—as well as thousands of lives lost because of the U.S.-backed Contras. And now this terrible hurricane.

The sadness that I felt then continues to this day. I know that suffering is not God's will for us. Wars are caused by greed and lack of love for other human beings. People cause wars, and people must stop them. Natural disasters will continue to happen because our wonderful earth is not something static but forever changing.

For me, the bottom line is the gift of faith. With faith I can echo Julian of Norwich: "All shall be well and all shall be well, and all manner of things shall be well." But believing this does not wipe out my sadness.

When my retreat ended, I returned to Managua, where more terrible news awaited me. The newspapers reported that there had been an ambush of a passenger vehicle near my village of San Juan. Nine people had been killed, five injured. Our Managua office asked me to get the names straight because the two leading newspapers had conflicting information.

The road to San Juan was washed out in several places where Hurricane Joan's fury had extended inland. Three times I climbed down and up steep ravines to change transports. Six hours later I arrived in San Juan, a trip of less than 50 miles.

There I learned that the Contra ambush of the passenger vehicle had occurred in broad daylight, only six or seven miles from town. I was aware that had I returned to San Juan a day earlier I could have been on that transport. The residents of San Juan were very shaken by the ambush.

When I asked Hortensia who had ambushed the vehicle, she said, "The Contras." That was something for her to admit, for her leanings were towards the Contras.

The next morning I went to the mayor's office to see if he knew the names of the people who had been killed or wounded. Although he didn't know the names, he told me that of the 17 people on the transport, nine had been killed, five were injured (three seriously), and three were unharmed.

I then went to the Sandinista office and talked to a very pleasant man who gave me the names of all 17 people who had been on the transport. The injured had been taken by ambulance to the hospital in Esteli. Of the three people not injured one was a nurse, who had now survived her second ambush.

Because I wanted pictures of the ambushed vehicle, I hitched a ride to La Dalia, a coffee plantation not far from San Juan where the transport had been taken. Bullet holes punctured the steel frames, both doors, and the windshield. The transport was the newest arrival on the lot filled with broken and bullet-ridden vehicles, the legacy of years of ambushes. What a sad sight and on what a sad note for me to be leaving Nicaragua.

The back of the public transport where 17 people were ambushed. If I had returned to San Juan one day earlier, I might have been on that transport.

My time with Witness for Peace was coming to an end. I packed my things, ready to leave in case any vehicle was going to Esteli. I said goodbye to friends and arranged to have lunch with Myra from the mayor's office. As we were walking to the comedor a pickup truck went past. Myra asked the driver where he was going. He said, "Esteli." I asked if I could go with him. We stopped for my backpack and at noon in the middle of the week I left San Juan de Rio Coco for the last time.

I felt bad about leaving San Juan so abruptly, but again it was the reality of life there. No mode of transportation ran on schedule. It could be days before any vehicle appeared in San Juan, the time of its arrival or departure known only to the driver.

On my way to Managua I stopped at the hospital in Esteli to check on the people who had been ambushed. I learned that the injured had been transferred to Managua. A three-year-old boy had died.

The next day at the WFP house in Managua, I started to pack up for the trip home. I felt good—but my weight was down to 85 pounds from about 110. I couldn't maintain my weight on a diet mainly of beans and rice.

The Sunday before I left Nicaragua I went to church at Santa Maria de los Angels. After about 30 baptisms I realized that there wasn't a 9 a.m. Mass, only baptisms. I took the opportunity to photograph the beautiful, brightly colored wall murals, paintings of the life of the common people. The painting behind the altar in the front of the church had caused a big uproar among some people. Christ on the cross is pictured as a peasant. Those not happy with the painting think that it is Christ pictured as a Sandinista. I guess that one sees what one wants to see.

My eight-month commitment as a team member with Witness for Peace ended in December 1988. After living in the war zones of northern Nicaragua, I was changed forever. I came to see things differently, my compassion for people deepened, and I listened with different ears and read with greater understanding. I put renewed energy into working to change unjust systems—a gigantic task—but I can't think of a better way to spend my life.

With mixed feelings I left Nicaragua. The happiness of going home was mixed with the sadness of leaving a people struggling against great odds to be free to govern themselves without outside interference. For them that struggle continues to this day.

Only recently I came across Dorothy Day's comment in the preface of her book on the life of St. Therese: "The work that Elizabeth, Mary, and I were engaged in—was to publicize and raise funds for General Sandino, who was resisting American aggression in Nicaragua. Our Marines were hunting him in the mountains. I did the publicity."

I must say that I am delighted to know that Dorothy had a connection with Sandino.

Center for Victims of Torture
A Good Rounder-upper

When I returned home to Minnesota the end of January 1988, I spent a couple of months slowing down and getting readjusted to the life in the U.S. Grocery store shelves stacked high with food and excessive goods in department stores were a vivid reminder of the injustice of life. Clean tap water, a luxury denied most of the world, I now used sparingly.

I then began the search for a job. After several weeks of interviews with parishes for a social justice coordinator position, I concluded that the job market was not clamoring for a 61- year-old white-haired woman. So I had to ask myself, "What am I going to do with my life? What would be meaningful and feed my soul?"

My answer to that question came when I was asked to do interpreting for a Guatemalan woman living with Sister Rose Tillemans, who ran Peace House, a community day center where poor and homeless people can gather to share stories and pray together. The woman was a client at the Center for Victims of Torture in

The Center for Victims of Torture in Minneapolis. Clients receive counseling at the center, but don't live there.

Minneapolis. From her I learned about the Center and its need for volunteers.

I called the Center and asked for information on their volunteer program and later met with the Center's volunteer coordinator. I told her that I wasn't suited for any of the things on the Center's help-needed list: typing, filing, computer work, library help, secretarial work, and general clerical assistance. However, I said was a good "rounder-upper," if such a person were needed. She assured me of the need. I attended classes for the new volunteers, thus beginning seven wonderful years of working with clients of the Center for Victims of Torture.

I learned that the mission of the Center is "to provide direct care to survivors of politically motivated torture and to the members of their families." Of the more than 400,000 victims of torture living in the U.S, an estimated 30,000 live in Minnesota. These survivors carry the burden of unspeakable, indelible memories. Unfortunately, the Center can handle only 150 clients a year.

When torture survivors arrive in U.S., they often live with a relative, friend, or a friend of a friend. One man told me he checked the phone book at the airport for a name common in his country in the hope that someone would take him in.

As a "rounder-upper" of clothes, furniture, household articles, and other materials, I was soon involved in the lives of the clients. Most of the clients I came to know were from Africa, and arriving in Minnesota in the winter was especially hard on them. After months of appointments related to housing many of the clients finally got their own living quarters. Because the apartments were unfurnished, the clients needed everything.

As a "rounder-upper," I needed a storage area and strong helpers. I already had a van. I soon located a building with a "For Rent" sign on it. I called the owner and explained who I was and what I needed. He told me that the building leaked, but he had space in the garage area of an apartment building that he owned. I could have two heated rooms for free. The "he" proved to be Keith Heller of my old Free Store days some 25 years ago!

The smaller of the two rooms needed shelving for household articles, so I called the Shaw Lumber Company, which had helped us out years ago at St. Joseph's House. I explained who I was and that I needed some odds and ends of lumber to make shelves.

"I'll send a man out to see what you need," said the pleasant voice on the other end of the line. The next day a fellow showed up, measured the room, and a few days later returned and assembled sturdy shelving on two walls. All at no charge.

Because I needed help lifting the larger furniture donations, I went to the Catholic Charities drop-in center and announced that I needed two men to help me. I would pay cash.

Geno, a solidly built Indian man, and Chas, a tall blond fellow good at packing furniture, became my helpers for years. They told me stories of their insights into street life, and I especially enjoyed Geno's quiet sense of humor. One day while delivering a load of furniture, I was expounding on the injustice done to migrant workers. "There she goes again," commented Geno. "Last week it was Indian fishing rights."

News via the grapevine travels fast. There was hardly any place I went that somebody didn't have something to donate: pots, pans, dishes, lamps, beds, bedding, chairs, desks, or couches (I will never move another hide-a-bed!). My van was seldom empty, and the contents of the storage area changed constantly.

Besides being a "rounder-upper," I sometimes located places for the clients to stay until they were able to obtain their own apartment or a more permanent location. Sisters of my community and the Franciscan Brothers of Peace were gracious in their hospitality. One client from the Center has become a permanent member of the household of one of our sisters. Many women from the Center have been welcomed at Sarah's...an Oasis for Women, a ministry of the Sisters of St. Joseph, which opened in

1996. Sarah's "provides hospitality for women seeking housing, community and safety on a temporary basis."

In my work at the Center I first thought I could use my Spanish with the clients, but during the seven years I was there I had contact with only one Spanish-speaking client, Maria, a former member of the Las Madres in El Salvador, who had known Archbishop Oscar Romero. Las Madres were mothers who spoke against the actions taken by an oppressive government.

One of Maria's tasks with the Las Madres had been to take photos of dead bodies found in the streets and garbage dumps and then try to locate the relatives. The families themselves could not claim the bodies, because it was too dangerous. One morning Maria found three decapitated bodies on the steps of her workplace.

The clients I came to know were well-educated and often spoke two, three, or even four languages. They came from Ethiopia, Togo, Somalia, Liberia, Cameroon, Eritrea, Bosnia, and Kosovo. A few were young university students, while others were lawyers, geologists, writers, teachers, and media people. They had been community leaders in their country and so had been targeted by the repressive regimes of their countries. All had been interrogated and tortured and were now trying to get their lives and families back together.

The clients were hard workers. When they finally got their work permits, they often held two jobs in order to have money to bring their families to the U.S. They seldom if ever found jobs for which they were trained. Instead, they handled luggage at the airport, did janitorial work, cleaned motel rooms, or worked in the parking lots downtown.

I never asked the clients about their personal lives or why they had fled their countries. Gradually, however, they would share with me bits and pieces of information about their lives. A woman told me of being forced to watch while her daughters were raped, and she herself was forced to hike through the jungle and cook for the soldiers. She had been beaten with rifle butts until her legs were broken. A thin young man described how, as a young 12-year-old, hot oil had been dripped on the back of his neck. He showed me the scars.

One of the clients asked me if I could arrange a prayer service for his father who had died. In his country the custom was to have a prayer service on the fortieth day after a death. The young man was not Catholic, but his father had been. He arrived at church with two of his friends dressed in their beautiful African robes, along with an interpreter. After Mass he placed a candle and a picture of his father on the altar, which was draped with a colorful African cloth. The interpreter read a touching story the man had written about his father's life. Later I learned that the African authorities had been looking for my client, who was here in the U.S. Because they had failed to find him, they killed his father.

How does one live with memories like these? Through my work at the Center and through reading its literature, I have learned that such memories will never go away but will continue to recur in dreams and flashbacks. Sometimes seeing such seemingly innocent articles as a cigarette, pencil, or jumper cables can bring back memories of being burned, poked in the ear, or shocked. The simple question "What is your name?" can at times cause a disturbing reaction in a client because that question was asked repeatedly while the person was being interrogated during torture. Although the memories will never go away, healing does happen through the counseling the men and women receive at the Center. As one client put it, "My torturer told me that no one will believe me. I know now that he was wrong."

As my months at the Center turned into years, I was privileged to be included more and more in the lives of the clients. I have been invited into their homes for meals, and I have joined in their celebrations when they graduated from college, when they got married, and when their family members finally arrived in the U.S. Once, after a marvelous meal, the hostess took the women guests into her bedroom and explained to us the different dresses that were worn in her country and how to wear them.

One afternoon I was invited to a special meal of goat meat, which a pregnant woman shares with her women friends close to the time she is to deliver. The goat feast, a custom of her country, is held so that the woman will have a safe delivery and a healthy baby.

I have learned that silverware is not essential for eating. Zewditu, a woman from Ethiopia, came to my apartment with the proper ingredients to show me how to make alicha, a dish of spiced ground meat or vegetables. This and other foods are picked up and eaten with a flat bread called budena.

Locating food native to their countries and cooking with a stove used to be a problem for many clients. Today many local stores sell foods found in the client's native countries, and cooking problems have been lessened.

I cannot put into words the richness that I have experienced from the people I have met through the Center for Victims of Torture. In sending holiday cards the clients never use my first name but address me as aunt, mother, or grandmother—all titles I cherish—as I am blessed with this extended family.

9

The Trial and SOA
"I sentence you to six months"

During the time I was working with the clients from the Center for Victims of Torture, I became acquainted with the Veterans for Peace. Each November since 1995 the Veterans have organized a bus trip to Fort Benning, Georgia, to protest the School of the Americas (SOA), located on the base.

People from across the United States gather at Fort Benning yearly to ask our government to cut the funding of the SOA, a combat training school for Latin American soldiers. According to the United States Truth Commission, more than two-thirds of the 60 officers cited for the worst atrocities during El Salvador's brutal civil war were alumni of the SOA. Nineteen of the 26 soldiers cited for the massacre, in November 1989, of six Jesuit priests, their housekeeper and her daughter, had received training at the SOA.

Information on the SOA and the track record of its graduates was spreading. Father Roy Bourgeois, founder of the movement to close the school, had speaking engagements across the country, including Minneapolis. Hearing his message heightened my knowledge of the SOA and sparked my resolve to get involved in closing the school. So in November 1996 I boarded the Veterans for Peace bus that was filled with Minnesotans and headed to Georgia. There we joined a group of 500 protesters gathered at the entrance to the base.

During our bus ride to Georgia, I had mulled over whether I should risk arrest by crossing the line onto the base. I was 69 years old, all members of my immediate family were dead, and I had no pressing obligations. Still, I wavered back and forth many times about this decision.

Should I cross this white line at Fort Benning, Georgia, and risk being arrested?

After I arrived in Columbus, Georgia, when I saw the crowds, heard the songs and speeches that stirred my soul and brought vividly to mind the atrocities committed by SOA graduates, I knew I had to act, and I was at peace with my decision. I crossed the foot-wide white line and entered Fort Benning with 59 other protesters.

The road into the base winds through beautiful grounds, tall trees, and gently rolling hills. As we rounded a bend in the road, military personnel were waiting for us and escorted us to two waiting buses. We were driven farther into the base to an area that was apparently used to hold errant soldiers.

This is the gate at the entrance to Fort Benning where the School of the Americas (SOA) is located. the gate is closed, guarded, and barbed wire is stretched across the top.

Left, the closed gate becomes a fine place to hang crosses and other meaningful symbols.

Tables for processing us had been set up in an old metal quonset hut. While we waited our turn, we were free to wander in a small area surrounded by a fence topped with barbed wire.

The process took such a long time that I grew concerned about getting back to the bus and my ride home. I was the only one from Minnesota who had crossed the line, and

Rain or shine, protesters come to Fort Benning. From left are Sisters Marguerite Corcoran, Jeanne Wingenter, Theresa O'Brien, Joanne Turgeon, me, Betty McKenzie, Kate McDonald, and Rose Marie Blazek, and consociate Gayleen Touhey.

I wondered if the bus would leave without me. I wouldn't have blamed my companions if they had left. I was delaying a whole busload of people who were anxious to start the 24-hour trip back home.

When we finally returned to the main gate, the sky was dark. With joy I saw two people from the bus sitting by the gate waiting for me. Amy Danzeisen and Sister Marguerite Corcoran had forfeited their supper to welcome me back. The bus driver and his passengers were off getting something to eat so the bus wouldn't have to stop later on. Silently I blessed the two by the gate, and the whole busload, for waiting for me. Everyone was understanding.

In 1996, Carol Richardson and I stand behind a Witness For Peace banner at Fort Benning.

After I arrived home I began my waiting, unsure what the consequences of my actions would be. Because it had been my first arrest, I figured I might get a two-month prison sentence, but I got a "ban and bar" letter. A certified letter from the Department of Defense dated May 1, 1997, stated: "You are hereby excluded from the Fort Benning Military Reservation for a period of five years from the date of this letter."

Nevertheless, the following November 1997, I again went to protest the SOA. This time 2,000 protesters gathered in front of the stage at the entrance to Fort Benning. They were young and old, men and women from many parts of the U.S. Their banners and signs displayed the group's diversity but unity of purpose. People from many different religious denominations and organizations marched, sang, and prayed together.

After songs, speeches, and personal stories by people whose lives had been directly affected by SOA graduates, those who were to enter the base and risk arrest were asked to come forward.

Six hundred and one U.S. citizens came forward, crossed that now infamous white line, and entered the grounds of the base. Of the 60 who had received the "ban and bar" letter the previous year, 25 of us were among the 601 crossing the line.

The walk into the base was a tremendously moving time for me. Each of us carried an 18-inch white cross bearing the name of a person who had been killed or "disappeared" in Latin America. My cross bore the name of Dorothy Kazel, an Ursuline sister, one of the four U.S. church women who had been murdered in El Salvador by SOA graduates in December 1980.

That cross had been handed to me the previous year by the organizers of a march at the Pentagon to protest the SOA. On the Pentagon lawn several protesters had dug shallow graves that resembled the graves in which the four church women had been found. Those graves in El Salvador, shown on television years before, had been burnt into my mind.

In November 1997, I cross over the line at Fort Benning, carrying the cross bearing the name of Dorothy Kazel, an Ursuline sister, one of the four U.S. church women who had been murdered in El Salvador by SOA graduates in December 1980. The other CSJs are Kate McDonald to my right, Marguerite Corcoran behind me, and Brigid McDonald to my left. Marlys Weber took the photo.

Now, eighteen years later, I was finally getting around to doing something about those deaths.

Two by two we wound our way through the beautiful green hills to the cadence of a slow drum beat. As the names of the people whose crosses we were carrying were called out over a loud speaker, we all answered "presente." Sitting somewhere among those green hills was an unknown flute player whose sweet melody floated gently through the rolling hills.

At the head of this prayerful, silent procession eight symbolic black coffins were carried representing the six Jesuit priests, their housekeeper and her daughter. The coffins contained petitions from thousands of citizens asking our government to stop funding the SOA.

As we rounded a bend, we could see police officers standing with their legs apart in a line across the road. Buses were parked in a long line on the right. The police ordered the coffins to be placed on the ground and our crosses placed inside them.

We were then loaded into the buses and driven farther into the base where tents had been set up in a large field for the processing. On the bus we were asked to surrender all lethal weapons, such as nail clippers, fingernail files, ballpoint pens, and slogan buttons. Our "weapons" disappeared into a large plastic garbage bag, never to be seen again.

A large waiting area had been roped off where we milled around waiting for our turn to be processed. Finally, we were frisked, ten at a time with our hands on a wall and our legs apart. Then we were moved to tents where we filled out forms, were fingerprinted, and photographed. Plastic bands were snapped on our wrists. The 25 of us "repeaters" got a blue band and a letter, a summons to appear in court on the following Wednesday morning at nine o'clock.

That was a jolt! Several people from Minnesota were among the 601 of us who had crossed the white line, but I was the only "repeater." I knew then that I wouldn't be returning to Minnesota with the others.

The relationship between the army personnel on the base and the protesters had always been respectful, and on this windy, chilly day they provided us with a meal of either chicken or ham. Some of the group declined the offer of food, but I was of the opinion that it was much better to use government funds to feed us than to pay for the training of foreign soldiers.

By the time we were driven back to the entrance of the base it was dark. The two buses from Minnesota were waiting, everyone anxious to start the 24-hour trip back home. I retrieved my duffel bag from the bus, waved goodbye to my traveling companions, and went in search of a place to stay.

I knew that several people from New York wore the blue plastic band on their wrists and were staying in the large motel near the entrance to the base. I knocked on doors until I found them. Nick Cardell, a 72-year-old retired Unitarian minister with a white mustache and a black cowboy hat, gave me his sleeping bag, and I slept on the floor with several others. Their place became our headquarters for the next few days.

On Monday, when our lawyers arrived, we plotted our strategy. Three of our group of 25 decided to plead "no contest," which meant that they would be sentenced right away and would start their prison sentence, if they got one, earlier than the rest of us. Hearing their sentences would give the rest of us an indication of what we might expect.

On Wednesday morning, the 25 of us gathered in the courtroom. One by one, the three who were pleading "no contest" stood before the judge and eloquently told him why they had crossed the line and entered the base.

When the three had finished speaking, the U.S. magistrate looked at all of us and remarked that he didn't know why on earth we would do such a thing as to enter the base. He advised us that if we wanted to close that base, "we should write our congressman." He hadn't a clue about what had been going on for years. Every person in Congress had been repeatedly written to, faxed, e-mailed, and talked to personally.

He then sentenced each of the three to six months in a federal penitentiary and fined them $3,000 apiece. The magistrate's name, ironically, was William Slaughter.

We were stunned into a collective silence. This was the first arrest for each of the three, and they had received the maximum sentence allowed for a misdemeanor. We now knew what likely awaited the rest of us who would have our trial in January.

Before we left the courthouse, we were again photographed and fingerprinted and then returned to our homes across the U.S. to await the letter summoning us for our court date.

Those few days in Georgia were very hard on me. I didn't know anyone in the group except Roy Bourgeois, whom I knew only slightly, so I felt alone. Also I realized that I probably would get a six-month prison sentence. I wondered what would be the reaction of my community, the Sisters of St. Joseph of Carondelet.

I was 99.9 percent sure that they would support me, but that .1 percent kept floating through my head like a dark cloud.

I was not only alone but very tired. I had arrived at Fort Benning at noon on Saturday after a 24-hour bus trip from Minnesota. The following day I had been arrested, and for three nights I had slept on the floor. During the day the 25 of us had planned trial strategy with our lawyers. On Wednesday morning we had gone to the trial, and late that afternoon I left for home. I hitched a ride with two of the men in our group who were going to Kansas City, Missouri.

We drove all night and arrived in Kansas City just before dawn. After a pancake breakfast the men dropped me at the Greyhound Bus Depot. I arrived at the Minneapolis bus depot about supper time, very tired but very glad to be home. I was extremely happy and grateful to see a group of my friends who were there to welcome me. And that dark cloud of possible nonsupporters dissipated quickly during the following days as I felt the love and support of my wonderful community and of other friends.

On January 6, 1998, two months after the first three protesters were sentenced, I received a certified letter that read as follows:

UNITED STATES OF AMERICA
vs.
RITA J. STEINHAGEN
You are hereby advised to appear before the
United States District Court for the Middle District
of Georgia, Columbus Division U.S. Courthouse,
U.S. Post Office Building, 12th Street at 2nd Avenue,
Columbus, Georgia, on Tuesday, January 20, 1998,
at 09:00 a.m. at which time you will have a trial on
the charges against you. If you do not appear at the
above time and place, a summons and/or arrest will
be issued forthwith.

Pitting the United States of America against me seemed a bit lopsided. However, since an "arrest warrant would be issued forthwith" if I did not "appear at the above time and place," I cleared my calendar and joined the other 21 people who had received a similar notice.

Four sisters of my community, Rose Marie Blazek, Marguerite Corcoran, Rita McDonald, Joan Wittman, and Joanne Tromiczak-Neid from our Justice Office, flew to Georgia with me on January 19, 1998, to attend the trial. A large group of supporters had come to the airport with banners and signs to see us off. It is hard for me to express the deep gratitude and thankfulness that I felt for them and for the many others, especially my community, who had supported me.

The trial began the next day, January 20. The scene in that courtroom is forever etched in my mind. Twenty-two of us co-defendants sat on wooden chairs in two rows to the left in the front of the courtroom. Ranging in age from 23 to 72, we were equally divided into women and men, and we were from a wide range of backgrounds: veterans, potters, musicians, ministers, social workers, college professors, priests, grandparents, nuns, graduate students, Catholic Worker members, and retired business people. We came from many parts of the U.S.

On a raised platform to our left sat Federal Judge Robert Elliott, who was to try and sentence us. Judge Elliott had been a sitting judge for a long time. He was 89 years old and looked to me like a benevolent great-grandfather. Although elderly, he managed to ascend to the presiding chair unassisted and sat there with a more or less pleasant expression, surveying his courtroom and occasionally cracking a little joke.

Judge Elliott was the same judge who, in 1974, granted a habeas corpus petition to Lt. William Calley that set aside the lieutenant's conviction for ordering a massacre of peasants in My Lai, Vietnam. This decision was later reversed. Judge Elliott also, in the 1960s, issued injunctions forbidding Dr. Martin Luther

King's civil rights marches in his district. An SOA Watch fact sheet stated, "In the 60s, Elliott, a strident segregationist, had seen most of his civil rights decisions reversed by higher courts."

Two long tables stood directly in front of us, one for the three prosecuting attorneys and one for our three defense attorneys. To our right was the packed courtroom, whose first floor and balcony was filled with our wonderful supporters, peace activists, friends, nuns, priests, and family members.

The trial's first day dealt with the dimensions of the base, the width of the entrance, and how far one building was from another. A prosecuting attorney had the engineer who designed the base explain it all to us. Why a day was spent on such facts was beyond me.

On the second day, January 21, the judge again cracked a few jokes and seemed quite benign. Father Roy, sitting behind me and sensing my feelings, leaned forward and whispered, "Just you wait." That was the voice of experience speaking. Roy, appearing before this judge now for the fourth time, had already spent more than three years in prison for sentences handed to him by Elliott.

Discussion that day was spent on the fact that we had crossed the white line and entered the base. Fort Benning is an "open base," meaning that anyone is free to walk in or to drive through the grounds—unless they are in disagreement with the training taught there.

The closing arguments of our skilled lawyers were so eloquent that I was sure we would be acquitted. But in the midafternoon the judge asked us if we had anything to say before he sentenced us. Of course, we all did.

One by one, as our names were called, we went to the microphone and gave the reason for our action. This was the most moving time of the trial for me as I listened to 21 intelligent, articulate, passionate people tell their stories. I then watched as each one of our group walked across the front of the courtroom to stand in front of Judge Elliott, who said in his southern drawl, "I find you guilty, and I sentence you to six months in a federal penitentiary and a $3,000 fine."

It was surreal. Peaceful, nonviolent people were being sentenced to six months in a federal prison for a misdemeanor. When Ruthie, a young member of our group, told the judge that she was indigent and couldn't pay the fine, he said to her, "I have here a form. If you sign this form that you won't enter that base again, we can waive the fine." The judge had obviously made up his mind about us even before the trial began.

The same offer was extended to each of us. One in our group said, "I haven't accepted a bribe since I was ten." Another told the judge, "It sounds like 30 pieces of silver to me." The judge had no takers.

When my name was called, Sisters Gina Webb, Mary McGlone, Maureen Freeman, Helene Wilson, and Marie Damian Adams—the leadership

The new leadership team of the Sisters of St. Joseph, representing our four provinces. The team's first excursion of "togetherness" was to attend my trial. From left are Sisters Maureen Freeman, Marie Damian Adams, Gina Webb, Helene Wilson, me, and Mary McGlone.

team of our St. Joseph Congregation, located in St. Louis—stood up in solidarity with me. Their standing deeply touched me, I will never forget it. Of course, they were immediately told to sit down.

According to the court records, part of what I said is as follows: "I am here today because I know of great injustices that have been inflicted on those small countries of Latin America. I have lived in Guatemala and Nicaragua, I have seen the suffering of these people. I am also here today, especially, for the four United States church women who were brutally raped and murdered in El Salvador in 1980. Five of the Salvadoran officers cited in that case were trained right here at the School of the Americas.

"The graduates of the School of the Americas are notorious for their cruelty, often raping and torturing before they murder. An editorial in the New York Times in September 1996 stated: 'An institution so clearly out of tune with American values should be shut down without delay.'

"For the past six years I have worked with clients from the Center for Victims of Torture, located in Minneapolis, Minnesota—some of them come from countries whose personnel have been trained here at the School of the Americas. I have seen marks of torture on their bodies, and I have heard their stories.

"I am appalled and I am ashamed to know that in some sense, I am the cause of their suffering and their pain because it is my country that is training their soldiers and it is my tax dollars and your tax dollars that pay for the training of these soldiers."

At the end of my testimony I spoke directly to the judge: "Your Honor, I have never been in prison. Today, on my 70th birthday, I suspect I will get sentenced. I guess that's a new stage of my life. But I tell you: I am more fearful of what is going on in this country than I am of going to prison. It is an absolute outrage when people such as we, and the people supporting us, can sit here and listen to what has gone on in this courtroom today. I am scared of what is going on in this country. I don't know what else I can do about it, but, believe me, as long as I live, I will do my best."

As I was leaving the courthouse after my trial, someone asked, "What did you get for your birthday, Rita?" I said, "Six months!"

I, like the other defendants, was sentenced to six months in a federal penitentiary and a $3,000 fine. After the trial, someone asked me, "What did you get for your birthday, Rita?" I answered, "Six months."

Twenty-two defendants now scattered across the United States to our homes to await the letter informing us to which prison we would be sent and our entry date.

A large group of wonderful supporters was again at the airport to greet me and my five companions as we returned to Minnesota. A reporter asked me why I would do an action that would result in a prison sentence. I answered, "You wouldn't be here talking to me if I weren't going to prison. I could make a thousand phone calls or write a thousand letters to my congressperson. That would generate no media attention, neither here nor in Washington. Unfortunately it takes a more drastic action to get people's attention."

I must admit, however, that I was unprepared for and astonished at the amount of attention a six-month prison sentence and a $3,000 fine would generate. Two fundraisers were held for me that gathered hundreds of friends, neighbors, relatives, community members, and people I didn't even know. I also was greeted by people that I hadn't seen since grade school. It was great affirmation and wonderful support for what was to come.

When I told the clients at the Center for Victims of Torture that I was going to prison for six months, they

In November 1998, more than 7,000 people gathered at the gates of Fort Benning, Georgia. Martin Sheen is one of the leaders of the procession into the base.

were terribly upset. To them the word prison conjured up the suffering they had endured while in prison in their own country. My description of a minimum-security prison did nothing to allay their fears. I assured them, however, that I would be back in six months.

10

Pekin Federal Prison
"I'm an inmate too"

T he letter I received from the United States District Court, Middle District of Georgia, on March 4, 1998, had advised me of my destination:

Dear Ms. Steinhagen:
This is to advise you that we have received notification from the Bureau of Prisons of the location designated for you to begin service of your sentence. For service of this sentence, you are instructed to report to the Pekin FPC, P.O. Box 7000, Pekin IL. 6155-700, 309/346-8588 no later than 2:00 p.m., on March 23, 1998.

I called the prison several times before I finally got instructions about what I could bring with me. I could bring a Bible but not underwear; all clothing and any medications would be furnished; and I would be prisoner 88119-02.

The trip to Pekin began the day before my required entrance date. Some sister

A gathering of sisters and friends came to see me off to prison. The sign was made by the people at The Bridge.

My sendoff from the St. Joseph Administration Building in St. Paul was a gathering of friends and supporters.

friends had gathered at the apartment of my friend Rose Marie for coffee, doughnuts, and a blessing before we walked across the street to the St. Joseph Administration Center in St. Paul, the point of departure. A large group of well-wishers had gathered on a beautiful Sunday morning to see me off (I asked them why they weren't in church!). With their blessing and good wishes I left for prison. My community's leadership team, Sisters Ann Walton, Maggie Kvasnicka, and Margaret Belanger, were my chauffeurs.

We stayed Sunday night in Peoria, Illinois, and late Monday morning we arrived at the prison entrance to find several carloads of people were waiting for us. They were parked on the edge of the road a couple of blocks from the prison because they were not allowed on the prison grounds. Sisters of my community from St. Louis and Peoria had come as well as other well-wishers. Brad, a reporter from KARE-11, a Twin Cities TV station, was there to capture the scene on videotape.

The group sang and prayed while I held a beautiful candle. The images on the candle, drawn by Sister Ansgar Holmberg and carved by Sister Gerrie Lane, depicted a cross raised above the School of the Americas and the likenesses of martyrs Bishop Oscar Romero, Jean Donovan, Sisters Ita Ford, Maura Clark, and Dorothy Kazel, Father Stan Rother, Brother James Miller, the Jesuit priests Ignacio, Amando, Joaquin, Segundo, Juan, and

Segundo, Elba their housekeeper, and her daughter Celina.

In the words of Sister Ansgar, the image also depicts "countless unnamed and mourning women whose blood is

The approach to Peking Federal Prison. The bleakness is permanent.

streaming down and nourishing the earth and all people. The murdered Christ is here in the person of these people. He is risen, too, in these same persons, and He keeps the hope of liberation alive. In them God has visited us." This prayer service was, for me, a powerful, blessed moment.

Only the car driving me to the prison was admitted on the prison grounds. We parked in the visitor parking lot. Sisters Ann, Maggie, and Margaret walked with me to the main entrance of the prison. Five guards or prison officials were at the door, and two came forward to escort me in. My sister companions were not allowed to enter, so I hugged them all, said goodbye, and entered the federal prison.

Then came the prison processing. "Nothing allowed in," said the fellow at the desk, although my Bible and watch got in legally. I went with a female guard to change clothes. When the two of us were in a small bathroom, she told me to strip naked, squat, and cough. She handed me my new clothes: white underpants and bra, two T-shirts size XXL, two dull green shirts and pants, white socks, and black steel-toed boots. Everything was too big for me.

Back at the desk I was told that I couldn't keep my calcium and asthma inhaler although both were new and in sealed containers. My small comb I happened to slip in my back pocket. The clothes and personal belongings I brought with me were boxed to be sent home. More photos and fingerprints were taken. My picture with my prison number was encased in a small plastic holder that was to be carried with me at all times.

Meanwhile, Brad from KARE-11 TV waited in the visitors' room. In my drab prison garb with boots too big and pants too long I stood before the camera and repeated the story of why I was in prison. The interview finished, I donned a heavy, ugly, gray-ish-green jacket and was escorted to my housing unit by Mr. Z., my case manager.

As I struggled with the big mesh laundry bag containing an extra set of clothes, a pillow, a couple of sheets, and two thin blankets, a door of the cafeteria opened, and an inmate shouted, "For gosh sakes, carry it for her." And Mr. Z. did.

Our destination was one of the two housing units called Kansas and Nebraska. In the Kansas unit he dropped the mesh bag on the floor of a small dormitory and left without a word. The dormitory had six metal bunk beds with no ladder to the top bunk. I selected a lower bunk and began to unpack the bag when four women came in and greeted me with a cheerful "Welcome, sister." I asked them how they knew I was a sister. "Oh, we have been waiting for you," they replied. "We have known for a month that you were coming, and today the media came."

Newspaper articles about me had been sent to inmates from their families in Minnesota. A few days later I was greeted as "Rita the Repeater," a term lifted from an article by Doug Grow published in the Minneapolis Star Tribune.

The women who welcomed me also brought gifts: shower thongs, lotion, small packs of coffee, deodorant, cookies, and a brush. Later I learned the gifts had been purchased at the prison commissary by women who were paid 12 cents an hour. The women knew that the commissary was only open at certain times and that the money I had brought with me would not be available for several days. I was deeply touched by their warm and kind welcome.

Later I observed that this kind of welcome was common. My two "companions in crime" for protesting at the SOA, Sister Mary Kay Flanigan, OSF, and Judith Williams, a grandmother, arrived in the early afternoon, and the same gift-giving was repeated, as it was for all other new "admits."

My new home was called a "bus stop." I would be there until there was an opening in one of the four wings, called "alleys." My steel bunk bed had a two-inch mattress on a metal slab that resembled a morgue autopsy table. Our beds were to be made in military style, all tucked in tight, and the schedules posted were in military time.

The notice on the hall bulletin board was probably a permanent one:

Pleased be advised that all beds should be made in Military Style Type Fashion. If you do not know how to make your bed in a Military Style Type Fashion please request a demonstration. If your bed is not made in Military Style Type Fashion a DISCIPLINARY ACTION will be taken. See perfect example of Military Style Type Fashion. A colored photo is Posted.

I wondered who wrote the "Military Style Type Fashion" notice—and how it could have been left hanging there so long. But then I observed a lot of "Military Style Type People" on the staff.

The rules and regulations of the place I learned from other inmates. I was startled to be told excitedly by the women in the dorm to "stand up, stand up!" It was 4 p.m., the time for a very important head count. All inmates were counted at 4 p.m., 10 p.m., midnight, 3 a.m., and 5 a.m.

The counts at night were taken by guards with flashlights making sure the bumps in the bed were inmates, not pillows. On weekends an extra count was made at 9 a.m. During the times I had visitors, the other inmates and I stood against the wall in the visiting room to be counted. I suspect that this counting is more of a maneuver to embarrass than anything really necessary.

The prison was situated in an open field, and the March weather was cold and windy. The jackets issued to us were ugly but warm. At night I slept with mine, placing it under me if the slab got too hard or over me if I were cold. Tough luck if it was both at once.

Each inmate had a metal locker. On the inside of my locker door were many slightly raised and hardened deposits of something white. The women told me it was toothpaste the previous occupants had used as glue to hold up pictures of their loved ones.

The prison routine started with breakfast at 6 a.m., but much earlier for kitchen workers. The cafeteria, although large, could not seat all 300 inmates at one time, so meal times were staggered. The place was always crowded and noisy. Some people SHOUTED rather than talked, even if the person was sitting across from them. I never got used to the noise. Meal time was not relaxing. I told Mary Kay that if I were going to lose it, the cafeteria would be the place. Of course, the place was so noisy that no one would notice if I did lose it.

The hall outside the bus stop served as a recreation area where the women played cards or just hung out. A good portion of the wall between the bus stop and the hallway was glass, so we had a good view of each other. I soon learned that the women were not on a regular schedule and that many preferred LOUD recreation late into the night.

After six weeks in the bus stop, I was moved to one of the four wings called alleys. A long cinder block room, the alley housed 32 women. Partitions five feet high and spaced at intervals along either wall created small alcoves open to the center aisle. Each alcove, originally built for one occupant, now contained two metal cots, two short metal lockers, one small desk, and a metal folding chair. The cots were one yard apart.

During the afternoon count, two rows of inmates, 16 in each row, stood facing each other while two guards, one at a time, walked between us, down the aisle and back. If their numbers tallied, the guards called headquarters to report the count. If the tallies differed, they counted us again.

My new quarters in the alley were not any quieter. The cubicle next to me was a gathering place for several silly women who never shut up, and the cinder block walls did nothing to absorb the noise. Laughter, shouting, and talking echoed through the place. The noise was one of the hardest things for me in prison. I was thankful that the TV room was a separate space.

Usually during her first few weeks in prison, a new inmate is not assigned a workplace. This gave me time to wander the grounds and check out the library, classrooms, gym, and the grey cinder block room used for a chapel. I located the commissary, clinic, and administration offices. Signs posted between the buildings read: "OUT OF BOUNDS, OUT OF BOUNDS, OUT OF BOUNDS."

Slowly the reality that I was in prison seeped into me. I was no longer free. The warden told us, "You go beyond those signs, you have climbed the fence." I was learning that the loss of freedom is a terrible thing.

After I had been in prison a month, a great sadness came over me. I was sitting on one of the wooden benches near my housing unit and looking across the grounds at the women sitting on farther benches or walking around like robots—aimlessly, hopelessly, sadly. Prison was simply warehousing people.

I was assigned to a small building where 14 inmates attended a class on word processing. My job was to correct their spelling and punctuation, an assignment that amused me greatly because I am a horrible speller. Luckily, a teacher's manual was provided.

After our workday, mail was distributed. All letters were opened before prisoners received them. Prohibited items, such as stamps, crocheted crosses, and Polaroid pictures, were removed and the letter stapled shut. How I hated those staples! I broke my fingernails trying to open my mail.

Mary Kay and I were both embarrassed at mail call because the greatest number of letters usually went to us. The letters I received amazed and humbled me. Large manila envelopes came stuffed with letters and drawings from grade school children. High school and college students wrote me letters. I heard from Methodists, Lutherans, Presbyterians, Quakers, Disciples of Christ, and Unitarians. I heard from priests, bishops, an archbishop, people who knew me in grade school, and other people I had never heard from before.

Photographer Dick Bancroft and his wife, Debbie, at whose place I often fished, sent me one of Dick's photos along with a picture of Marv Davidov, my fishing partner, sitting in a canoe holding up a huge sunfish. I pinned both photos to my bulletin board and found myself wishing I were fishing!

I heard from Kip, a fellow I had met 30 years ago when I was working on the West Bank in Minneapolis. He was now a hermit and trapper, living in the north woods of Minnesota. Letters arrived from 14 countries, and I was amazed and heartened to receive a letter from the Zapatistas in Mexico. The Zapatistas are members of an indigenous movement interested in justice for the people of Chiapas.

Letters came from all branches of the Sisters of St. Joseph and numerous other orders of sisters from all over the world. One letter that touched me deeply came from two Sisters of St. Joseph from the Albany Province whom I didn't know. Their kind letter came from Kenya, where they were working, and really brought home to me the connectedness of all of us.

I had this overpowering realization that what one does is never done in isolation. We are one body. We give love, support, and encouragement to each other even though we might not know one another personally. Of the thousands of letters that I received, only one person wrote to express disapproval of my actions. The letter was not signed.

Paperback books were allowed in prison as were hardbacks, if they were sent directly from the publisher. How surprised and pleased I was when Elizabeth Johnson, CSJ, professor of theology at Fordham University in New York City, had her publisher send me a copy of her new book, Friends of God and Prophets. The section on hope in her book touched a chord in me, for I saw hope played out among the women: "In times of peace and blessing, hope gives thanks and expects further good. In times of affliction and distress hope, still directed towards God, longs for deliverance—genuine hope grows in strength as the situation grows more desperate, becoming 'hope against hope' that refuses to give trouble the last word because ultimately God's mercy will encompass it with care and new life."

I saw a lot of "hope against hope" in prison, which is such a deadening place. Many of the women were hoping against hope because they refused to be swallowed up or crushed by the system.

A variety of religious services were held almost weekly, usually in the evenings, and I attended most of them. The Catholic Mass was at noon on Thursdays. The priest was at a different place theologically from Mary Kay and me, and eventually our differences surfaced.

Occasionally Mary Kay and I were readers at Mass, and Judith Williams played the small organ (which she managed to repair). Being accustomed to using inclusive language, we adjusted the readings to include everybody and made God more accessible by not being strictly male. Eventually our adjustments led to a heated sermon denouncing any trifling with Holy Scripture.

"It is very plain that God is Father, as Jesus said, 'I and the Father are one,'" we were told. "We must be obedient to the Pope, bishops, and priests, as they are the direct descendants of God Almighty."

Mary Kay, the reader of the day, explained after Mass that she had been using inclusive language for 14 years. "You should repent," said the priest.

One day after Mass one of the women said to me, "You know, the priest is always praying for the Pope and vocations. Why doesn't he ever pray for prisoners and justice in the prison system?"

Most of the women were in for some type of a drug offense and none of the women told me that they were innocent. But they did tell me that what they had done didn't warrant the appalling long sentences that they received. Often, for a first-time, low-level drug offense, the sentences were six, eight, ten, or more years.

I had the feeling that most of the women were often just one thin layer away from crying—and there was much to cry about. Prison is such a screwed-up place, and the longer I was there, the more the stupidity of it all hit me.

I watched the women walking around and around or sitting on the wooden benches smoking cigarettes. They had no place to go, and their work assignments were usually "busy work." The gym gathered those who were into bodybuilding or occasional line dancing. At times I used the stationary bikes if I could find one that worked. Broken bikes were no longer replaced. The TV room was seldom empty. Late at night and into the early morning hours women knitted or crocheted while the television programs continued nonstop.

The turnover of inmates was slow but steady. One day a new woman was "self surrendering" at the side entrance. Three carloads of people came with her. Much crying and hugging took place at the door where she was to enter. Many of us inmates watching this scene were much moved, and a few women were crying, no doubt reliving the day they had entered that same door.

When Martha was leaving the prison, a woman who taught a knitting class at the prison brought her a few daffodils (it is amazing that the flowers were allowed in). Martha brought the daffodils to our unit. I could have cried to see such beauty in the stark surroundings. Beauty is so essential for the soul.

Finally, the bleakness of late winter gave way to spring. Early one morning, seeking quiet time, I went to the walking path on the other side of the gym. I stood still, watched, and listened. Dandelions dotted the grass, and a pheasant called. The birds, running around in quick little steps, reminded me of sandpipers. Their song was a gift that cheered me.

Dawn lifted my spirits, but what fed my soul and lifted my spirits the most was the incredibly beautiful evening sky. Pink, orange, blue, mauve, yellow, and violet were often painted on the huge dome of sky above us. The colors slowly shifted positions as if doing a slow dance. God was telling me, "I will provide the color and beauty needed for your soul."

Of course prayer was also needed for my soul, and I found many of the women very prayerful. At 9 p.m. each evening a group of black women gathered in a prayer circle in the chapel. I asked Nadine, one of the women who attended, if the circle was only for black women, as I never saw a white woman in the group. "No," she said, "all are welcome."

Mary Kay and I went with Nadine and continued to go to the prayer meetings. We sang songs, read scripture, and prayed for the women in prison, their families, the staff and their families, world needs, and especially the women going through a hard time because their "out date" had been extended. We always ended with the same prayer: "May the Lord watch between me and thee, while we're apart one from another..."

We attended other prayer meetings, too. Sister Jean, a Franciscan from Peoria, periodically conducted a small prayer group in early evenings. She joined Mary Kay and me at supper one evening and told us how scared the staff had been about our coming. She had been told that we were not to lead prayer meetings, that she was to remain in control.

I wondered what the staff thought would happen if Mary Kay or I had led the prayer meetings. Well, we didn't lead prayer meetings, but we did pray with the women and the needs they asked us to pray for.

One day during Holy Week I sat at one of the picnic tables on the other side of the gym. Slowly I read the Stations of the Cross sent to me by Maurilaurice, a parishioner of the Church of St. Stephen, my parish in Minneapolis. The beautiful prayers touched me deeply.

Holy Thursday was very special. Four Jewish inmates invited Mary Kay and me to attend their Jewish Seder meal. Fran, the leader, had been born in Israel, and Hebrew was her first language. The six of us sat around a small table in the room used as the chapel while Fran read volumes of prayers in Hebrew at top speed. After the prayers we shared a meal of tender beef strips flown in frozen from Florida and heated in the prison oven, all arranged by a rabbi.

Holy Saturday brought welcome visitors from St. Louis: Sisters Mary Damian and Helene. I told them about the volume of mail I was getting and how bad I felt about not being able to answer all the letters. They suggested the idea of a "Rita Watch" newsletter as a way to answer most of my mail. I would cut the return address off the letters I received and send them to Mary Damian and Helene. They would have Sister Winifred (Winnie) Adelsberger create a mailing list for the newsletter. My CSJ community in St. Paul, with the help of Jackie Kelcher, one of the administrators at the St. Paul Province offices, offered to do the same thing. From that time on the bulk of my mail was answered through "Rita Watch," a letter I wrote every couple of months.

The Mass on that beautiful Easter Sunday was sparsely attended; however, a Protestant service held in the gym attracted a large group of women. The inmates could invite family members to the Easter service. I sat on the bench outside of my housing unit and watched the visitors, escorted by an inmate, on their way to the gym. When the last of the parade of visitors, dressed in their Easter finery, had entered the gym I crossed the yard and joined the service.

After Easter I was back at my work assignment, correcting papers of the women in the business course. For seven and a half hours, five days a week, I sat in that small room but didn't do two hours of work a week. The teacher had a high shrill voice that she used at full volume. Very hard on my head.

My work assignment did have one advantage, however. The teacher, who was from a college in Peoria and not from the Bureau of Prisons, allowed me to read or write letters during class, something not allowed the inmates who were supervised by prison personnel. The teacher came to class one day with a beautiful bouquet of lilacs whose beauty and fragrance seeped deeply into my grateful soul.

The lilac bouquet reminded me of a notice I had seen on the bulletin board regarding Mother's Day. "Ladies, keep in mind that you will be allowed to receive only a one-stemmed flower during the weekend. No bouquets of flowers, not a dozen roses, not a vase. Not a basket of flowers, but a simple one-stemmed flower."

I thought about that notice. Oh, why just one flower? Imagine the joy of seeing a whole bouquet of flowers. Imagine the beautiful colors and smells in the housing units. And why no vases? But thank God for the one flower, and the women would find some plastic thing to put it in.

Each day, when class was over, I went to my sleeping quarters for the very important 4 p.m. count. Being counted several times a day was an unpleasant reminder that I was not free, at least as far as external circumstances were. But no prison can control my inner freedom. This truth is stated on one of my T-shirts, one that I didn't happen to have in prison with me: "You can jail the resisters—but you can't jail the resistance.'"

This daily counting of inmates prompted a haiku:

Counting the humans
Prison guards, key chains clanging,
Pass inmates standing.

Each day after the count I headed for the cafeteria or, occasionally, I joined the commissary line. I checked the articles I wanted on the list of things available at the prison store and waited my turn to slip the list through a slot in the wall to an inmate who would fill the order.

One day while I was standing in the long commissary line, a woman in the back of the line hollered to the woman behind me, "Elsie, how many people ahead of you?"

Elsie shouted back, "Two inmates and a nun." The women in the line cracked up.

I turned to Elsie and said, "Elsie, I'm an inmate too."

"Naw," she said, "you are a visitor passing through."

I liked the women and often heard stories that were both funny and sad. Elena, a Mexican woman from southern Texas, had been a truck driver. She didn't want her 90-year-old mother to know she was in prison because "she would die of a heart attack." So whenever Elena called her mother, she was always "on the road" someplace.

Elena also made beautiful paper flowers, and I asked her to teach me how to make them. I figured that when I got out, making paper flowers would be more socially acceptable than the other things I was learning.

From the women who were doing time for forgery, I had a lesson on how to forge checks. Former gang members taught me how to flash gang signs. Practicing this newly learned skill produced gales of laughter in the cafeteria or elsewhere.

Other women gave me advice. I was told that I was government property and, if I got so sunburned that I needed medical attention, I would be destroying government property. That sure got me thinking. I knew that destroying government property was a bigger offense than what I was in for. If I got six months for a misdemeanor, I better stay out of the sun!

Sylvia had worked for a big-time drug dealer who operated only on weekends and by appointment only. Buyers were mainly doctors, lawyers, clergy, and CEOs. The dealer sold only cocaine and often made $7,000 on a weekend. Sylvia was a "mule" (a drug carrier) who went to Florida or Texas and smuggled the drug back in a balloon inserted in her vagina. "You know," she said, "about a big as a baby." She knew that if the balloon broke she would probably die.

Life's sorrows carried an extra burden in prison, where there was no place to grieve privately. Three Hispanic women came to get me one evening. Maria, another woman, had received a letter informing her that her brother had been killed in a car accident in Mexico. The four of us sat with Maria in a classroom until we were told it was 8:30 p.m. and time to lock the room. We moved to one of the benches outside in the public area. After the three women left, I sat with Maria until the 10 p.m. count time. It is hard to grieve so publicly.

One evening in an alcove not far from me, a woman was crying and sharing her story with her roommate. Of course, we all could hear her. Part of her pain was, "and they (her family) think that I am on vacation at some kind of resort when this place is so hard."

Her words reminded me of Psalm 30:

> At nightfall, weeping enters in,
> but with the dawn, rejoicing.

Hopefully, hopefully.

I loved the dawn. Sitting in blessed silence early one morning behind the gym, I watched the sun come up in all its splendor.

> Orange red the east
> Morning chorus of song birds
> Singing up the sun.

Moments of peace, quiet, grace, and—yes—joy.

The quiet of the early dawn was a time to ponder my life. I wondered what my parents, now long dead, would think about their daughter, dressed in prison garb and housed with 300 other inmates. I think my mother would have understood better than my dad, who, with a questioning look, would have tilted his head slightly and gently shaken it.

On hot, muggy weekends many of the women "went to the beach." Wearing their commissary-bought T-shirts and shorts and toting a bag filled with oils, lotions, and drinks, they headed to the cement basketball court. They lay on their skimpy towels and got various degrees of sunburn. That scene caused a great sadness in me. It would be years before many of those women could trade that hard cement for a sandy beach.

Those hot days often produced wild storms at night. After one such storm, the morning was hazy and I went before breakfast to a bench behind the gym for peace, quiet, and prayer. In the early morning haze I watched the slowly changing cloud formations.

Steel blue clouds stretched
above gently rolling hills
swallow rising sun.

The days might start out peacefully but, at times, it is hard to maintain balance in prison. Incidents like temper flare-ups can have dire consequences. Inmates guilty of saying or doing anything unacceptable to the staff are sent to the county jail in Peoria, which had a reputation among the women for terrible conditions and bad food.

Twice I was threatened with being sent to Peoria. The first time happened when I was being searched before entering the visitors' room. I had a small scrap of paper on me containing five words to remind me what I wanted to ask my visitors about. The guard was furious and reported me to my unit counselor, who called me over while I was visiting with my friends. I explained what the words on the paper meant and then said to her, "Isn't this whole thing silly?" I heard no more about the incident.

The second time I was threatened with the Peoria jail the angry guard shouted at me, "You have the right to remain silent, anything you say can be used against you!" I learned that someone at the prison had fished out a large manila envelope that I had mailed, on behalf of another inmate, to Sister Gina Webb in St. Louis. This woman was working on her legal case and needed five photocopies each of 95 pages. Using the prison copy machine would have cost her ten cents a copy, a price she could not afford. I had called Gina, who said she would be glad to help the woman.

All of this was perfectly legal, yet the woman, owner of the legal papers, was also screamed at and threatened with being sent to Peoria. Finally, after three weeks, when the matter got straightened out, I paid another pile of postage money to send the papers to Gina.

Although I wasn't sent to Peoria, I did get other raised-voice admonitions. One time the loudspeaker announced that I had visitors. When I went to the door of the room where we are searched before entering the visiting room, the door was locked. I went to the main desk to report this situation but was told in a LOUD VOICE that I must stay outside and wait until the door was opened. LOUD VOICE also told me I must tell my visitors that they cannot bring me food (my second notice on this issue). There should be a sign on the main entrance door, "Please don't feed the inmates."

Many prison rules seemed highly arbitrary, and examples of incompetence and inefficiency were plentiful. A woman who had been in our housing unit for two months was whisked away because, we were told, she had tuberculosis. All of the inmates then were lined up for Mantoux tests, a skin test for detecting latent TB infection. Three days later the woman was back. "She was the wrong person," someone said. Another said, "She didn't have it."

To me it was maddening. Another example of the Bureau of Prison's inefficient, screwed up system. The next morning I woke up angry. I was mad all morning and most of the afternoon. And there was no explanation to any of us about what happened or why she was sent back.

Of course, the prison staff didn't have to explain to the inmates why they made that decision or any other decisions—no matter how unreasonable they might be. Mary Kay had a woman visitor from Chicago on a hot summer day. The guard wouldn't let her in because she was wearing a sleeveless blouse. The visitor had to go the town of Pekin and buy a T-shirt to wear.

The leadership team of my community came to visit me. The team had made arrangements with the chaplain to visit me in the middle of the week. I was surprised at that and also that we would be visiting in the chapel, not the visiting room. We sat on metal folding chairs in the square cinder block room and visited—with no access to vending machines. But I was happy to see them: they were very supportive of me, as was the rest of my community.

A woman in the alcove next to Mary Kay and me told me that when we had visitors the guards often went through our belongings. We were surprised that the guards didn't disturb anything in our quarters because usually when an inmate's cell was searched the whole place was torn apart.

One thing the guards could have found in my cell was a sheet of paper sent to me by a friend with a list of things to do to relieve stress. One thing on the list was, "if it is not delicious, don't eat it." I really laughed.

Walking was another stress-relieving item that was on the list. At times I used the walking path, but I didn't like the monotony of going around in a circle so I wandered aimlessly on the basketball court. When the women asked me what I was doing, I told them that I was "practicing the ancient art of meandering." Most evenings I had to be careful not to step on the hundreds of tiny toads that shared the court with me.

June was a hot, muggy month of tiny, flying insects that bit and got in my eyes, ears, mouth, and hair. June also was our halfway mark. We had three months to go. Mary Kay put a few little daisies in an old plastic pill bottle and perched it on my stand. I gave her a large sheet of blue paper, supplied by a woman in the educational supply room, to put on her bulletin board as a background for her pictures or cards.

The summer evenings were beautiful, but the weather could change rapidly. Once a big storm came up fast with heavy rain and a strong wind. An announcement told us to return to our barracks. The sky was black, but an hour later there was clearing in the west, and the sky turned weird shades of orange and green. And then fol-

lowed one of the most spectacular sights that I have ever seen: a huge, wide, brilliant rainbow that was actually two rainbows that stretched from one horizon to the other. The colors in the two bands were in the opposite order of the other. Many women were out looking up to

Sisters Avis Allmaris, Ansgar Holmberg, and Agatha Grossman visited me in prison. The cottonwood seeds that floated by while we visited inspired a haiku.

the heavens, including my friend Mattie, who said, "I thought the Lord was coming right down then to get us."

The following Saturday my friends Sisters Agatha Grossman, Ansgar Holmberg, and Avis Allmaras came to see me. We had a wonderful visit despite our empty stomachs (the sandwich vending machine was broken). When our blood sugars reached a critical low, the candy machine got my friends' money for a candy bar for each of us.

That Saturday, as we sat in the outside visiting area in the sun, we watched fluffs of cottonwood seeds sailing in the air. Their presence surprised me because there were no trees near the prison, but Ansgar said cottonwood seeds can travel far. Perhaps they came from trees by the river that I had been told was down the road a piece. Later, remembering those seeds, I wrote:

> Fluffs of cottonwood
> Sailing upward in blue sky
> In prison but free.

I missed trees and beautiful Minnesota so I was delighted when I called my friend Loie Orton in Walker, Minnesota, who said, "Come to the cabin when you get out." That joyful thought stayed with me as I anticipated the coming of my release date.

Getting visitors cheered me and helped get me through my prison sentence.

My friends Char Madigan, CSJ, (left) and Rita Foster, CSJ, journeyed to visit their imprisoned friend.

I am blessed with smiling friends from home, (left) Joänne Tromiczak-Neid, CSJ justice coordinator; Joan Wittman, consociate; and, on my left, Rose Marie Blazek, CSJ.

Mr. Z., my case manager, also was aware that my exit day was approaching. One day I was called to his office where he explained that it was his duty to collect ten dollars from me, which the government wanted for processing my paper work. I told him that I was mad at the government and didn't want to pay it. He replied that if I didn't pay it he would have to give me a "shot" (a disciplinary write-up) and put me back in the bus stop, although he said he didn't really want to do it "because the inmates would riot."

When I asked if there were other options, he told me that there were none and suggested that I talk to Mary Kay and Judith about the matter. I had until Saturday to pay the money.

After consulting with my two friends, the three of us went to Mr. Z. on Saturday and told him we didn't want to pay the ten dollars. When asked if he could just waive the fee, he replied that his superiors would not allow it. Still, he said, he didn't want to send us back to the bus stop, and besides, his mother had told him "to be good to the sisters."

"Good advice," we said.

The matter went unresolved for another week, until Mr. Z. asked to see us again regarding the money. After some hemming and hawing, he said that he had figured out something, and we wouldn't have to sign anything. He had found a solution. We told him to say "hi" to his mother.

Toward the end of my prison stay my nephew, Tony Steinhagen, and his wife, Tracy, came from Green Bay, Wisconsin, to see their relative in prison. As far as I know, I am the only member of our family who has "done time." That's pretty good, considering that one in every 141 residents in the United States is in prison or jail.

Other visitors towards the end of my time were Edwardo and Rosa, whom I met in the 1980s while working at Annunciation House in El Paso, Texas. Edwardo told me a story that deeply touched me and hit directly on my reason for protesting the

SOA. He had been in the army in El Salvador and had been given a list of people to "exterminate." In the first house on the list, a man came to the door, a small child sitting on his shoulders and his pregnant wife beside him. Edwardo refused to shoot the man so the higher-ranking officer with him killed the man. Edwardo was jailed for refusing to shoot the man, but later escaped from jail. The officer who did the shooting and his commanding officer at headquarters, General Carlos Vides Casanova, had both been trained at the SOA (Vides Casanova was guest speaker at the SOA in 1985 and is now living in Florida).

My last "Rita Watch" was different from the others. In it I shared my anger at the prison system, which gives excessively long sentences to nonviolent, low-level drug offenders and replaces rehabilitation with punishment.

My last few days in prison were a touching mixture of sadness and joy. Connie, the gardener, gave me envelopes of flower seeds. Each envelope was marked with the name of the flower variety and the name of a person whose favorite flower it was. She said to me, "When you plant these seeds and they grow, pass the seeds on to other women, and each time that happens tell them to remember the women in prison."

The Spanish-speaking women threw a party, serving Mexican food and music, for Mary Kay, Judith, and me. On Sunday, at the Pentecostal service, the choir sang a farewell song for us. Marilyn, a woman from Minnesota, came to our cubicle to tell us how much she would miss us and how we had affected so many lives in so little time.

After the 4 p.m. head count Sunday, the women in our alley asked Mary Kay and me not to leave our unit. An hour later they placed a small table from the TV room outside of our cubicle. A new black plastic garbage bag, split down the seam, was draped over the table. Our farewell meal, prepared by our whole alley of 30 friends, featured commissary canned beef, chips, tortillas, cheese, beans, and a rice dish served with "kitchen connections" of lettuce, chopped tomatoes, and onions. All ingredients were piled on the plastic garbage bag and burritos were made and shared by all. Many of the women also brought us gifts they had made.

I cannot describe the rollercoaster of emotions I experienced: the joy of going home, the pain of leaving so many wonderful women behind, knowing that many of them had years left of their sentences.

After the Thursday noon Mass, the priest asked Judith, Mary Kay, and me to come forward for a special blessing, as he did for all of the women when they left prison. He said he knew that we had had a positive influence on the women and that they would miss us. Mary Kay thought that he had tears in his eyes!

After Mass we brought to Receiving and Delivery our nicely packed boxes containing our personal items to go home with us. There we had to unpack the boxes and put the contents on a desk. All articles were examined, counted, repacked, and taped shut.

Not much sleep Thursday night. By 7:30 Friday morning we were on our way down the walk to the door of the exit room. A large group of women walked with us. There were hugs and tears and singing. The prayer group that we attended in the evenings was singing my favorite song, "He might not come when you want Him, but He's always right on time."

On September 17, 1998, the day before we were released from prison, Mary Kay Flanigan, OSF, and I were again captured by the media. The cross necklaces we are wearing were gifts from an inmate. *Daily Herald photo/Bill Zars. Printed with permission.*

It was a wonderful yet bittersweet send-off, until the warden, Miss F., came out to disperse the group. We heard that she came back from her vacation a day early, no doubt to supervise our release.

More than a half-dozen prison staff were standing around as we made our exit. We first were driven next door to the nearby men's prison to collect any money we might still have in our account (the accounting system and the television were controlled from the men's prison). While we were there, the top warden came to greet us and wish us well. Back at the women's prison my driver's license was returned, and I was handed a Bureau of Prisons Program Review sheet, which stated that I had made an "excellent adjustment" to prison life.

The three of us piled our boxes on a cart and wheeled the cart to the cars that had come to pick us up. No other cars or media were allowed on the premises. Sisters Rose Marie and Annie were there to pick me up, as were the three members of my community's leadership team. A group of 30 or 40 other supporters parked their cars along the road and walked across the field toward the prison to welcome us.

There in a field we gathered, sang, prayed, and rejoiced in our freedom and then headed to Ernie's Cafe in Pekin for a bacon-and-egg breakfast and a cup of good coffee.

I felt great joy at being free—and also a great sadness at leaving friends behind. I recalled a very moving letter I had received shortly before my exit date, from the Metanoia Community in Florida, a community I knew nothing about. Part of the letter read as follows:

> The first full breath of freedom beyond the last door of the prison will be something you will cherish immensely and always remember. But, no matter how joyous that occasion, as you walk across the parking lot a piece of your heart will remain with the friends that you are leaving behind. There is nothing that anyone can do or say to lessen this pain for you.

The trip home with Sisters Rose Marie Blazek and Agatha (Annie) Grossman was wonderful. I was amazed at all of the trees and how green everything was, lush as a jungle. At 8:30 p.m., I was home, greeted by a big sign on my front lawn that read:

Rita, Welcome Home
Signed — Your neighbors

And soon to my little apartment, a wonderful bed—and blessed silence.

11

My Life Goes On

Just as there was adjusting to do when I entered prison, there was adjusting to do after I was released. I remember thinking, "Is it true, am I really free? Can I walk where I want to or go for a spin in my van?" These simple things, denied me for six months, validated my freedom— one of the terrible things lost when in prison.

One of my first acts as a free woman was to thank the gathering of sisters and friends who filled the large province community room to welcome me home. I thanked them for their letters, visits, and prayers, which had daily buoyed my spirit while I was in prison. I then went north with three companions to my friend Loie's cabin near Walker, Minnesota, for a few days of rest and relaxation.

When I came back to the Twin Cities, I had a large number of speaking requests. My time in prison had generated interest, and these talks gave me the opportunity to tell about the SOA. That's precisely why I, and more than 100 others, went to prison: for the opportunity to expose the training taught at the SOA and the track record of its graduates.

My prison sentence was another life-changing experience for me. Before being incarcerated, I never thought about prisons or prisoners. Today I have another passion besides closing the SOA: to do something about our so-called criminal justice system. People with health problems like drug addiction or mental illness do not belong in our jails and prisons. And the mandatory drug law often gives excessively long prison sentences.

I continue to work to close the SOA and am a member of a criminal justice working group. At times I join a Wednesday morning group that pickets at Alliant Tech Systems (ATK), a manufacturer of indiscriminate cluster bombs and weapons that use depleted uranium. Numerous people have been arrested at

ATK for peacefully protesting and have spent time in the Hennepin County workhouse. I was one of six who spent a week in the workhouse, a sentence that added to my prison education.

In 2002 I returned to Central America, this time to Guatemala. I received a call from Mary Lou Ott of the Nonviolent

After I was released from prison in September 1998, I continued to attend the protests against the SOA at Fort Benning for several years.

In 2000, the view from the stage of the 12,000 protesters gathered at Fort Benning. Father Roy's apartment can be seen on the far right. He is the priest who initiated the protests against the SOA.

Peaceforce asking me if I would go to Guatemala for three weeks to accompany a woman human rights activist whose life was in danger. Ideally, the presence of "companions" from outside Guatemala would serve as a deterrent to those who might want to harm these activists, as harming them would create international attention.

The situation in Guatemala is far from peaceful. Since the peace accords were signed eight years ago, there has been little success in bringing to trial those responsible for atrocities committed during the civil war. To date, there has been no compensation for the war victims. Recent attacks against

In 2001, I hung on the Fort Benning gate a picture of the four churchwomen—Maura Clark, Jean Donovan, Ita Ford, and Dorothy Kazel— who were murdered in El Salvadore by SOA graduates.

the protesters and the continued intimidation of human rights activists highlight the dismal situation in Guatemala

Although the situation there carried some small risk for me, the only time I really feared for my life was riding with the woman. She drove with one hand, constantly talking on the phone with the other, as we zipped in and out of congested traffic, barely missing buses and beggars.

In the last few years my energy level has been slowly decreasing but not just because of age. Three years ago I was diagnosed as having COPD (chronic obstructive pulmonary disease), and, in July 2004, I started using oxygen to help me breathe more easily. In November 2004, for the first time in eight years, I missed the largest protest ever held at the gates of Fort Benning.

Whenever possible I go fishing. Sometime I go alone, at other times I go with my fishing partner, Marv Davidov. I usually head for the home of Dick and Debbie Bancroft, on Sunfish Lake, a small lake south of the Twin Cities. It is a place of peace, quiet, and beauty that replenishes my spirit. I am

Fishing with Marv Davidov on Sunfish Lake. Both Marv and I are grateful to the Bancrofts for the use of their canoe and for letting Marv store his container of worms in their refrigerator. (Photo by Chris Spotted Eagle.)

most grateful for their friendship and hospitality. It is from their dock or canoe that I catch giant sunfish or bass.

My slowing down has given me time to reflect on my life's journey, an incredible trip. I am fortunate to have had good parents and a happy childhood spent in small towns.

The luckiest thing that ever happened to me, however, was to get hooked up with the Sisters of St. Joseph. Oh, I know it was the providence of God—not luck, but whatever you want to call it, the CSJs have been my support and encouragement for 55 years. They are an incredible group of women, and I am privileged to be one of them.

Joan Chittister, in her book The Fire in These Ashes, writes: "The purpose of religious life is not survival, it is prophecy. Don't wish your life away. There is work to be done in this period."

I trust that my Spirit companion will note my travel restrictions and will be content with local activities.